BEST-SELLERS
for
Fairs & Fêtes

The Australian Women's
Weekly
craft library

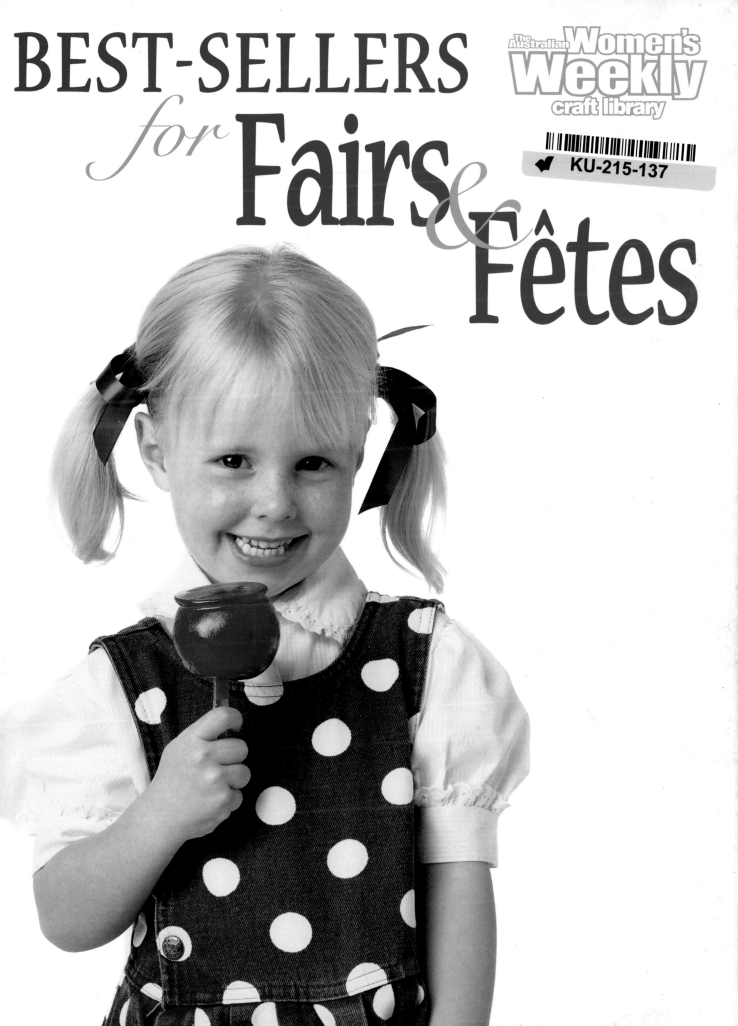

Acknowledgements

The publishers are grateful to the following contributors:

Maria Ragan for Dog & Cat Mats, p. 16, Aromatic Pot Mats, p. 19, Paper-covered Books & Mouse Bookmarks, p. 26, Mouse String Minder, p. 28, The Bag Bag, Mushroom Bag & Bath Sachets, p. 29, Fur Cushion & Hottie Cover, p. 35, Painted Cactus Pots, p. 41, Crocheted Finger Puppets & Lion Puppet, p. 46, Monster Money Purses, & Lounge Lizard, p. 48, Calico School Dolls (dressed by Georgina Bitcon), p. 49, Bungy Fish, Juggling Balls & Balloon Heads, p. 52, Pompom & Glitter Pencils, p. 54, Key Rings, Hair Toggles & Necklaces, p. 56, Bath Mitts, p. 59, Furry Picture Frames, p. 60, Furry Shoulder Bag, Photo Album & Pencil Case, p. 61, Rice Angels, p. 64, Country Angels, p. 65, Sequin Baubles, p. 66, Ham Bag, p. 68, Baby Santa Bib, p. 69, Victorian Soldiers, p. 71; **Pamela Worsdall** for Felt Bags, p. 6, Stencilled Boxes, p. 7, Terracotta Candle Pots, p. 18, Etched Bottles, p. 31, Tinfoil Stars & Gift Bags, p. 70, Stencilled Jam Covers & Tags, p. 89; **Lynda Maker** for Paper-covered Box, p. 7, Recycled Bottles, p. 8, Découpaged Pillboxes, p. 22, Fossil Tags, p. 33, Christmas Crackers, p. 72; **Jane Ulman** for Evening Bags, p. 21, Jewelled Pencils, p. 54, Lighthouse Quoits Set, p. 57, Braid-wrapped Balls, p. 67; **Vivien Prince** for Log Cabin Native Birds & Patchwork Glasses Case, p. 24; **Helen Lovass** of Nimble Thimble Studio, Melbourne, for Silk Strawberries, p. 23; **Anne-Maree Unwin** for Bread Dough Baskets, p. 30, Decorated Bottles, p. 31, **Mary Coleman** for Natural Packaging, p. 9, Pressed Flower Gift Tags, p. 26, Tussie Mussies, p. 39; **Mary Keep** for Tomato Pincushions, p. 15; **Mary-Anne Danaher** for Lavender Hearts, p. 14, Crazy Chooks, p. 17; **Gabrielle Collins** for Butterfly Wings, p. 50; **Susan Coates** for Dolly Peg Angels, p. 71; **Tonia Todman** for Birdseed Bells, p. 42; **Georgina Bitcon** for Rose Soap Balls, p. 12, Citrus Bath Oil, p. 13, Covered Coathangers, p. 20, Stencilled Sarong, p. 27, Bath Salts & Fizzy Bath Bombs, p. 32, Sprouting Head, p. 41, Cross Stitched Garden Gloves & Hand Balm, p. 43, Butterfly Antennae, p. 50, Fairy Wand & Tiara, p. 51, Cackling Chooks, p. 55, Kitchen Angels, p. 64, Pearly Star, p. 66, Potted Pomanders, p. 68, Dolly Peg Santas, p. 71; **Coats Spencer Crafts** for Knitted Menagerie, p. 47, Bunny Slippers, p. 58; **Australian Country Spinners** for Baby Footy Boots, p. 58; **Hayfield** for Knitted Balls, p. 58.

Special thanks also to the Australian Women's Weekly Test Kitchen and the school community of Annandale North Primary School, NSW.

Contents

Getting Started

Whether it's a charity craft stall at a shopping centre or a monster Spring Fair in the grounds of the local school, the key to a successful enterprise is always good organisation. So gather your wits – and a band of willing helpers – and draw up a plan of action.

Once you've decided to hold a fête, the first thing you need to do is form a Fête Committee, with a coordinator and helpers for every section of the event, such as White Elephant, Raffle, Books, Hot Food, Cakes, Craft, Entertainment, Garden, Kids' Activities, Chocolate Wheel and so on. Don't forget you will also need volunteers to keep records, organise publicity, set up and operate a public address system, check legal requirements regarding public liability and insurance, liaise with local authorities, seek local or corporate sponsorship and to act as treasurer. You can't assume that every member of your community will be as keen to help as you are, but enthusiastic recruitment should provide a solid core of people to run things. (If it doesn't, you might need to re-think the whole idea!) Provide an opportunity to help for those with less time or inclination by calling for money donations – and use this money as a working fund for expenses that will be incurred during the course of preparations.

Assuming the venue is settled, the next important thing is to decide on a date. Large functions can take up to 12 months' planning. Although it's perfectly possible to do it in less, do try to allow as much time as you can, or you will find yourself run absolutely ragged trying to get everything done in time. When choosing a date, try to avoid major sporting fixtures, such as Grand Final Day, or a holiday weekend. Check with your local council for date clashes, and check too with other local schools and churches in your area to avoid choosing the same date as their annual fête.

Don't bite off more than you can chew. In the first flush of enthusiasm, it's very easy to decide you'll have a jumping castle and a pet show, pony rides, fairy floss, face painting, a visit from the fire brigade, celebrity guests and more than 50 stalls. And by all means, have the lot – as long as there are enough people to help with the organisation. Otherwise, be realistic, or "Monster Fête" might come to have implications you didn't actually intend!

As far as basic equipment is concerned, you will need tables to display your wares. Trestle tables or fête stalls can be hired – check under *Hire – Party Equipment* in your business telephone directory. You'll also find public address systems, barbecues, jumping castles, mobile coolrooms, espresso machines, hot water urns, even toilets, should you need them.

Of course, all this will eat into your profits, so while it's probably a good idea to hire the tables (they're all the same size and they fit together nicely), you might be able to borrow other things, such as market umbrellas, barbecue equipment, folding chairs, maybe even a PA system. Consider publishing a simple Fête Newsletter every couple of weeks, in which you update everyone, list your generous sponsors, specify the meeting times of various sub-committees and ask for help with the things you need.

Enlist the help of the local business community, and when help is given take care that it is acknowledged. For instance, a local business might be prepared to foot the bill for printing flyers for your fête, as long as they can advertise on the back. If the village fruit shop donates a basket of fruit for a raffle prize, this information should be included with the prize. Choirs, a capella groups, orchestras and high school bands in your area will often be prepared to donate their time for a performance just for the exposure it gives them. Ask around – there'll be knockbacks of course, but you'll also be delighted by how generous most people are prepared to be.

If the fête is running all day, you'll want to serve food and drink – a welcome diversion for customers and an excellent way to increase profits. Cut some of the donated cakes and slices into single servings and offer morning and afternoon teas. If any of your volunteers are scone makers, you can also serve Devonshire tea, which is always a drawcard. The coffee should be real, if possible – if a hired espresso machine is out of the question, borrow lots of coffee plungers and make up pots as needed. Provide simple seating and tables and ensure some shade. For cold drinks, try an old-fashioned lemonade stall (see page 94) in addition to the more standard lines. It is lunch, however, that will probably be your greatest seller – who can resist the delicious smell of frying onions at the Sausage Sizzle? Start frying early; the smell makes everyone hungry and you will have customers from the moment you start. Sausages and hot dogs are the traditional way to go, but investigate the culinary talents of your volunteer pool – you might discover an irresistible souvlaki or Thai-style marinated chicken wing! The trick, when demand hots up on any food stall, is to work in a production line so that the food servers do not need to (and indeed, for hygiene reasons, should not) handle the money.

Perhaps the best bit of advice we can give is to learn from experience – other people's. Visit different fêtes, if you can, and see for yourself what seems like a good idea and importantly, what does not. In the course of research for this book, we've seen some terrific ideas. Now that desk-top publishing is so accessible, one school had compiled and illustrated its own cookbook of favourite recipes that was selling like hot cakes. Another was selling printed tea-towels featuring a tiny self-portrait of every pupil in the school. Yet another had organised what they called a Glass Jar Tombola. Every pupil had to bring to school a lidded glass jar of any size, filled with anything at all – lollies, biscuits, small soaps or cosmetics, mustard, vanilla beans, sewing things, a manicure set, a gift voucher for a book store, a pair of socks, small toys, jewellery, pencils, a pack of cards – the list is infinite. The jars were numbered and became the prizes in a lucky draw that ran throughout the day of the fête – perfectly simple and wonderfully lucrative.

One last thing – don't forget to make contingency plans in case it rains. We can't guarantee the weather, but we can promise that all the good things and ideas on the following pages will help to make your Big Day a brilliant success.

Perfect Packaging

Seasoned fête organisers know that you can sell almost anything if it is presented nicely. Without adding much to your total outlay, inventive packaging means you can increase your income, since not only are elegantly presented items more attractive to consumers, they also command higher prices.

A Clear Choice

Cellophane is the packager's dream! It is inexpensive, comes in a variety of colours as well as the traditional transparent, and is also available in a number of tiny prints and polka dots. Its great advantage is that the sale item remains tantalisingly visible whilst being protected from air, moisture, dirt and little fingers. The simplest way to use it is to place items on a large circle of Cellophane, then draw up the edges and secure tightly with curling ribbon. This method is ideal for whole cakes, plates of biscuits, slices and homemade sweets. To help support their weight, cakes can be placed on a circle of firm cardboard (recycle cartons and boxes) before wrapping. Use paper doilies or aluminium foil to line polystyrene meat trays (wash thoroughly first, of course), which are the perfect size for presenting biscuits, slices and sweets. Although readymade Cellophane bags are available in several sizes, they are more expensive than single sheets, so why not make your own? It gets rather messy using glue, but it's a quick and simple matter to zigzag the sides of a bag together on your sewing machine, using a colour that will complement the bag's contents. Tied at the neck with an organza bow, these bags are perfect for fizzy bath bombs (above, right). But not all packages need to be see-through. Decorated felt bags, such as those shown here, can be mass-produced in any size, and the humble paper bag can also be embellished with stencils, stickers or potato printing.

Boxing Clever

Boxes of all shapes and sizes can be recycled as pretty containers for fête items, so organise friends to start collecting them for you. There's no need to reject the ones with a brand name plastered all over the sides – this can be disguised in a number of ways. For instance, the pretty box (at right) once held something far less glamorous than scented bath bombs. We covered both box and lid with a sheet of textured paper (cut away excess at corners), then lined it with gold tissue and decorated the lid with a little organza ribbon, a rose bud and a tendril of gold beading wire.

The colourful star-stencilled papier mâché boxes were found in an unadorned state in a bargain store, but the painting treatment would also work for recycled boxes. The trick to getting good colour coverage is to start with a coat of white gesso, a special thick white paint that will cover a multitude of sins. When this coat is dry, you can add artist's acrylic in the colours of your choice, using the star stencil on the pattern sheet for decoration if you like. When the paint is dry, finish box and lid with a coat of water-based matte or gloss varnish.

Cups of Fun

Get the kids to help paint big bold stripes of acrylic paint on the outside of polystyrene drinking cups. They're great for presenting flavoured popcorn, as shown here, but also for other treats from the Sweets Stall. The whole thing can also be encased in Cellophane, if you prefer.

What's In A Name?

Labelling is important on handmade gifts, not only because it's nice for customers to know whether they've bought Three Fruits Marmalade or Lime and Ginger, but also because it provides an opportunity to add the pretty finishing touches that can make all the difference to whether a product sells or not.

Try labelling homemade food goodies with an inexpensive calligraphy pen (opposite, top left) – easy once you've had a practice run or two.

Investigate the wonderful range of rubber stamps in specialist stamping shops. There will be an appropriate one for almost anything you can think of and they can be hand-coloured to produce eye-catching labels (opposite, below, left and centre). Also available are stamps that say "Handmade from the Kitchen of …" or something similar, making a single purchase useful for a wider variety of products.

Pretty recycled bottles (opposite, top right) can be given an elegant new lease of life by dipping their corks in melted wax, winding the necks with silver string and adding tiny tags, cut from greetings cards and wrapping paper.

The unusual "fossil" tags (opposite below right) look lovely on coloured glass bottles of bubble bath. Simply roll white air-drying modelling clay (such as DAS) to 5mm thickness and cut into 5cm squares, rounding corners by hand. Press small objects (such as shells or seedpods) into the clay to make an impression, make a hole in one corner and allow to air dry. Paint with a watery mix of Yellow Oxide artist's acrylic, then wipe off most of the paint, leaving darker colour in the impression. Allow to dry, then thread onto raffia. Glue a tiny paper label to the back.

It's Only Natural

Hiding the labels on jar lids is easy. Cloth hats are an obvious solution, but to be a little bit different, we tied calico and hessian covers with raffia, then added cinnamon sticks, star anise, bay leaf labels (use a gold felt-tipped pen), small wooden utensils, fresh chillies and slices of dried orange. (Place four 6mm slices of orange on paper towel, cover with more paper towel and microwave on 50% power for about 8 minutes, turning half way through, changing towel when wet, and taking care towards end of cooking that they don't burn. Dry on racks.)

Gifts

The handmade gift stall is the heartland of all the best fairs and fêtes and should include a range of items for sale, both traditional and novel. The gifts we have included here are mostly things that can be made fairly quickly in numbers and, most importantly, at not too much expense. Of course, there will always be some outlay for materials but this can usually be minimised with a little creative thinking. Op-shops are a wonderful source of interesting fabrics and costume jewellery; manufacturers of clothing and bedlinen may be prepared to donate remnants; and waste recycling cooperatives such as Reverse Garbage (check your local business phone book under "Recycling") are treasure troves of inspiration and useful things — from fabric, leather and timber off-cuts, bits of haberdashery and faux gems, to signage materials and empty containers suitable for presentation and packaging.

The Good Oil

Tangy citrus bath oil is simple to make and appealing packaging will make it a sure seller. Gently heat 30g anhydrous lanolin (from a chemist), 2 teaspoons honey and 3/4 cup grapeseed or almond oil in a saucepan until just melted. Remove from heat, allow to cool until lukewarm, then add 1/4 cup vodka, 1 teaspoon lemon essential oil, 1/2 teaspoon orange essential oil and a few drops of clove oil, stirring constantly until well combined. Pour into small, pretty, sterilised bottles and seal. Decorate with a slice of dried orange or two (dry slices slowly on baking paper in a very low oven until completely desiccated), and add a tag that details how it should be used – a generous splash as the bath is running. The citrus stencil, shown on page 89, would also be ideal for decorating the tags.

Ring of Roses

Opposite: Present fragrant homemade soap balls in inexpensive papier mâché boxes painted in feminine pink and white candy stripes – don't fuss with masking tape; slightly rustic looks nice. A softly-tinted hand-stamped tag (deckle the edges with special scissors) provides a charming finishing touch. For mass production, the balls could also be presented in Cellophane bags, tied simply with pink ribbon and a tag. A sprinkling of rose pot-pourri in the bag is also a nice touch. To make soap balls, grate 100g plain, unscented soap into a bowl. (You can also buy finely ground unscented soap from some craft stores.) Add 3-4 drops red food colouring to 1/3 cup boiling water and pour over the soap. Add 6-10 drops rose geranium essential oil and mix well with a spoon. Leave to harden a little, then break off small pieces and roll into even-sized balls. Leave to harden further. When really hard, moisten your hands with a little essential oil and roll balls to add a final shine and smoothness.

The Colour Purple

Dried lavender is used to fill these charmingly simple scented heart sachets – easy to mass-produce from inexpensive fabrics, such as gingham, and perennially popular with gift buyers. Bulk dried lavender is readily available in craft and homewares stores. Using the heart outline, printed on the pattern sheet in a pink tone, cut two fabric Heart shapes and stitch together around the outer edges, allowing 5mm seams and catching in a fabric or ribbon hanging loop at the top. Leave a small opening in one side. Clip curves, turn right side out, fill lightly with lavender and slipstitch opening closed. Stitch a button to the centre of each sachet, stitching through both layers. For presentation, the hearts can be piled as they are in a rustic basket, or individually bagged in Cellophane with a hand-stamped and coloured tag – there are a number of delightful rubber stamps available featuring lavender that make mass-production a breeze.

Rich and Red

They look almost good enough to eat, but these luscious tomato pincushions are destined to grace a sewing box rather than the dinner table. Made from felt or fabric scraps, they're the perfect item to feature on a country crafts stall. Instructions are on page 95.

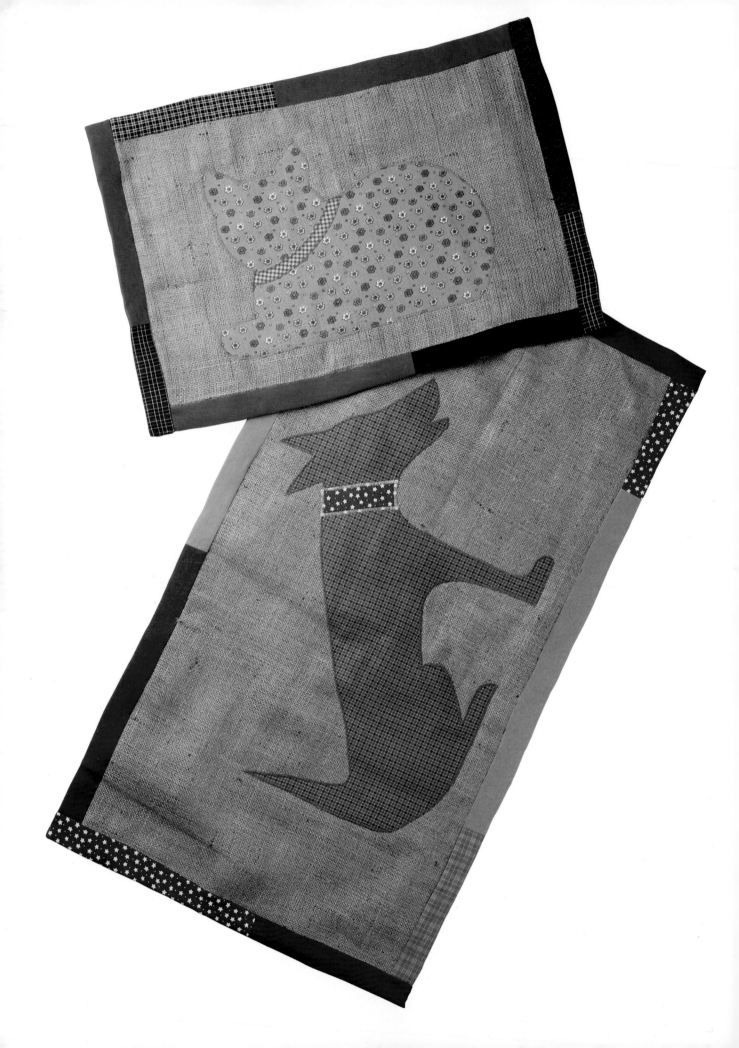

The Cat Sat on the Mat …

… and the dog can too! These handsome hessian pet mats are made in two sizes, for both Fido and Puss. If you are lucky enough to have access to empty hessian feed sacks, they make the ideal starting point. If not, natural (or perhaps coloured) hessian is a perfect and inexpensive alternative. From hessian or feed sacks, cut two rectangles per mat (90cm x 50cm for a dog, or 60cm x 40cm for a cat). Place the layers together, wrong sides facing, and bind the edges with 8cm-wide straight strips of fabric (3cm each side, plus 1cm seam allowance on each edge). This is a fantastic way to use up scraps, because the strips can be joined as needed for the required length. Bind top and bottom edges first, then the two sides, folding in raw ends to neaten. Using the appliqué outlines printed on the pattern sheet in pink, cut fabric shapes and baste (or *very lightly* glue with spray adhesive) to the centre of your bound mat. Using a narrow zigzag stitch, appliqué the outlines in place, adding details as desired.

Crazy Chooks

Novelty rice-filled chickens will bring a touch of country whimsy to your craft stall before going to new homes on kitchen dressers or mantelpieces. They would also make amusing companions for (and a delightful way to present) Easter eggs. Cut two 17cm x 20cm rectangles of velour fur fabric and stitch together with right sides facing, allowing 1cm seams, catching a triangular felt beak and a simple felt comb into the seam at appropriate places, and leaving an opening for turning. Turn right side out, clip corners, fill loosely with rice or lentils and slipstitch opening closed. Stitch black glass beads in place for eyes.

Let There Be Light

Bargain stores are often the source of great cheap materials for crafters. These tiny terracotta pots and plain pillar candles – both inexpensive in a local bargain store – are transformed into pretty and very saleable Tuscan-style table decorations with the addition of an easy painted border. Of course, any sized terracotta pot with a rim could be painted in the same way and citronella candles make a practical variation. Instructions are on page 95.

A Touch of Spice

When a hot dish or teapot is placed on top of these aromatic pot mats, a warm spicy fragrance fills the air. Two 20cm squares of fabric are joined with 5mm seams, then turned right side out and filled with a mixture of whole cloves, crushed bay leaves, crumbled cinnamon sticks, star anise, cardamom pods and a little ground cinnamon, nutmeg and cloves for extra fragrance. The spices can also be mixed with rice or polyester fibrefill to make them go further. As you can see, a basic square is only the start – a smaller square can also be bordered with contrast fabrics, if desired, or the whole square could be made from patchwork strips or squares, depending on the time and materials available. To help keep the filling evenly distributed, it is a good idea to stitch the square bag into channels before filling, or quilt it simply, or, as shown, use buttons to hold the layers together, after it has been filled.

A Hanging Matter

Nobody *ever* has enough padded coathangers and craft stalls are a traditional source of extra supplies. Like all the best fête items, they can be made from scraps in your fabric hoard. A pretty if not strictly necessary finishing touch is a tiny organza bag filled with pot-pourri. Instructions are on page 95.

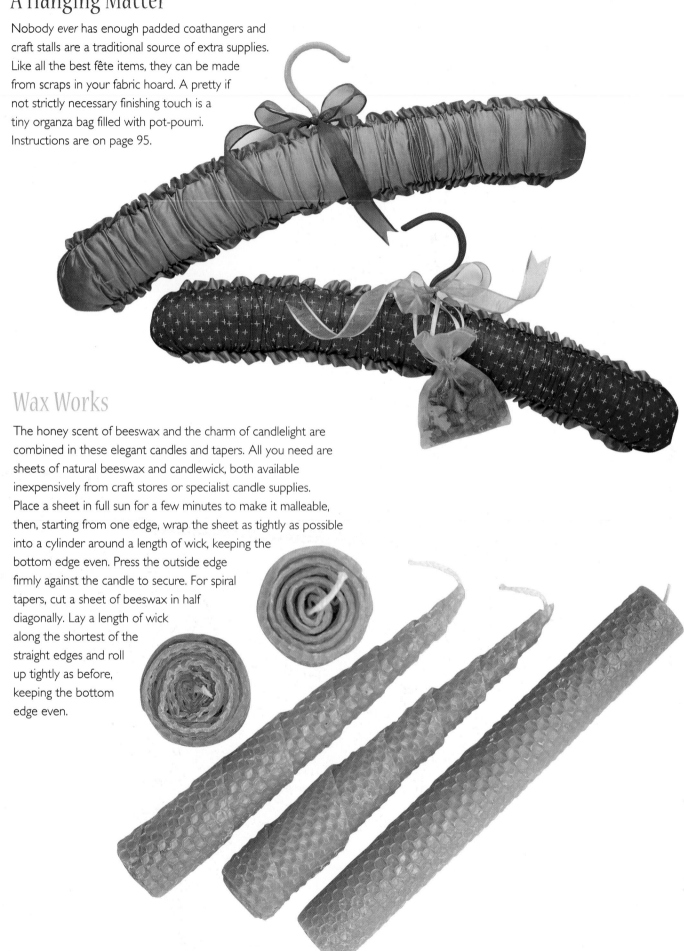

Wax Works

The honey scent of beeswax and the charm of candlelight are combined in these elegant candles and tapers. All you need are sheets of natural beeswax and candlewick, both available inexpensively from craft stores or specialist candle supplies. Place a sheet in full sun for a few minutes to make it malleable, then, starting from one edge, wrap the sheet as tightly as possible into a cylinder around a length of wick, keeping the bottom edge even. Press the outside edge firmly against the candle to secure. For spiral tapers, cut a sheet of beeswax in half diagonally. Lay a length of wick along the shortest of the straight edges and roll up tightly as before, keeping the bottom edge even.

Enchanted Evenings

Pretty jewelled evening bags and purses can be made for a fraction of the cost of store-bought ones. The secret to keeping the cost down is to haunt opportunity shops, bargain fabric stores and remnant tables. All are great sources of fabric off-cuts and remnants, faux jewels and decorative buttons, tassels, lace and braids – the only limit here is your imagination, not your purse. The simple lined bag, that can be made in any size and fabric combination, is decorated with whatever you have gathered – no two are alike. Instructions for making the basic bag are on page 96.

Tiny Treasures

These shiny pillboxes would make perfect little items for your gift stall – they're so easy to decorate that you can make half a dozen at once. Using small sections of wrapping paper (one sheet goes a very long way!) or even old calendars, our simplified version of découpage – forget the 20 laborious coats of varnish – results in a glossy surface that looks like a traditional finish, in a fraction of the time it usually takes. Instructions are on page 96.

Rich Pickings

Exquisite silk strawberries look almost as luscious as the real thing. Made from scraps of silk dupion, the pretty berries can be made up in a variety of toning colours or, of course, in red. Decorated with tiny gold beads and gold thread, they make charming ornaments for their own sake, but could also hang from a small pair of scissors or a chatelaine as a miniature pincushion, or be filled with lavender to scent drawers and linen cupboards. The white strawberry would also make a delightful keepsake for a bride. Instructions are on page 97.

22

Birds of a Feather

This delightful group of Australian natives will draw immediate attention to any stall where they happen to alight — and they're popular with children and adults alike. The **Galah** and **Lorikeet** can be made two at a time using a patchwork block known as Courthouse Steps, the **Sulphur Crested Cockatoo** is fashioned from traditional Log Cabin blocks — and the feathered fantasy **Love Birds** are for those in too much of a hurry to be doing any patchwork! All can be filled with rice to sit plumply on a shelf, or with polyester fibrefill to serve as colourful pincushions. Instructions begin on page 98.

Open and Shut Case

You might think that patchwork and mass-production are mutually exclusive but these pretty glasses cases are actually very quick to make in quantity by piecing, backing and quilting a large block of patchwork fabric all in one clever operation, then cutting it into sections for each case. Instructions are on page 100.

Threads and Patches

Popular Log Cabin patchwork again – this time featured on a simple potholder, with the traditional red square at the centre to symbolise the fire in the hearth. Of course, any fabric scraps can be used, as long as you sort them into "light" and "dark" to maintain the subtle shift in tone that characterises the block. With simple, rustic quilting, this is a charmingly old-fashioned yet eminently practical item for a gift stall. Instructions are on page 100.

Paper Chase

Ordinary cheap notebooks are given a new lease of life with pretty paper covers, using printed and textured rice papers. Simply cover each book as though you were covering school books, gluing the overlapping edges down on the inside covers. Now (this is the clever bit), mix one part PVA glue to three parts water and paint this mixture liberally over the rice paper cover on the outside of the book. Allow to dry. For a neat finish, glue the first and last pages of the book to the inside front and back covers, so that the raw edges of your new cover are concealed. A nice touch is to cover a pencil in paper to match, then tie the two together for presentation.

A Mice Idea

Suede and leather scraps are turned in a flash into endearing mouse bookmarks, complete with joggle eyes and whiskers. A bag of leather scraps can be bought from leather merchants, and sometimes from craft shops. Once the ears are slipped through two slits in the leather "body" strip, finishing the bookmark is a simple matter of gluing eyes and whiskers in place. The outlines for the mouse and ears are printed on the pattern sheet in black.

Pressing Matters

Manilla baggage labels and pressed flowers make a set of decorative gift tags that can be made for next to nothing. If you're in a hurry for your pressed flowers, consider investing in a flower press that can be used in a microwave oven (from craft and hobby shops) — it makes the job a breeze. Group the tags in packs of six and wrap in Cellophane for instant buyer appeal.

Sheer Pleasure

The two metres of fine Indian cotton for this pretty summer sarong or throw cost less than an icecream at the beach! Simply hem the raw edges then decorate the selvedges with shell stencils (printed on the pattern sheet in black), using fabric paint in two softly contrasting colours. If you prefer not to cut your own stencils, investigate the great range of pre-cut stencils available from craft stores, or use large rubber stamps, which also come in a variety of interesting motifs — don't forget to use a fabric ink stamp pad when stamping on fabric.

In the Bag

Here's a group of practical bags that no environmentally-conscious household should be without. For saving and recycling those endless plastic bags, there's **The Bag Bag**; for taking the ''mush'' out of storing mushrooms, there's the washable **Mushroom Bag**; for a good long soak in a hot tub there are calico **Bath Sachets** to hold bath salts, herbs or soothing oatmeal; and for keeping string on hand and untangled, there's a whimsical **Mouse String Minder**. All are tried and true fête sellers and can be made quickly and inexpensively in large numbers. Instructions begin on page 101.

Use Your Loaf

Plain salt dough – strictly non-edible – is moulded around oven-proof dishes to create these wonderful woven baskets. Once baked and varnished, they are perfectly sturdy and can be used as containers for dry food, but should not be immersed in water. Biscuit cutters are used to make smaller shapes which can be used to decorate the baskets themselves or to make traditional bread dough Christmas decorations. This is a project that the kids could help with, and all it takes is flour, salt and water. Instructions are on page 103.

Bottle It Up

Interestingly-shaped bottles and jars (get everyone to save them for you) can be recycled into elegant storage vessels with the addition of an etched design. We used a non-corrosive etching cream available in craft stores, to transform two bottles into these beautiful matching oil and vinegar containers – once applied, the finish is quite permanent. Instructions are on page 104.

Even quicker than etching, and equally as attractive – empty coloured glass bottles can be jazzed up with gold coloured liquid leading (look for it with the glass paints in craft stores). It may take you a couple of tries to get the leading looking right but mistakes can simply be wiped off while they are still wet. Corks of different sizes can usually be found in homewares stores or hardware shops. Decorate the finished bottles with raffia ties and a bread dough shape if desired, and fill with flavoured oil, herb vinegars or bathroom products.

Spring Shower

Perhaps nobody ever goes to a fête *expecting* to buy a shower cap but strangely enough, they seem to disappear as fast as the covered coathangers! This duo is destined to do likewise. Made from a pretty floral print and lined with plastic, both shower cap and matching toiletries bag are quick and easy to sew. Instructions are on page 105.

Coming Clean

The secret to marketing these homemade bathroom products (and almost everything else at your fair) is all in the packaging. Scented bath salts, bubble bath and fizzy bath bombs are all incredibly cheap and easy to make but they look a million dollars when they're packaged elegantly – and that means that not only are they more attractive to consumers, you can also charge more for them! Elegant presentation does not have to add dollars to your outlay, either – see pages 6 to 9 for clever packaging ideas.

To make **Bubble Bath**, combine 1 cup Epsom salts, 1/2 cup baby shampoo, 2 tablespoons glycerine and 2 teaspoons rose, lavender or lemon essential oil in a bottle; shake well to combine, then decant into pretty bottles and label.

To make **Bath Salts**, combine 1/2 cup Epsom salts, 1/2 cup rock salt, 6 drops essential oil, 3 drops glycerine, and a little food colouring to tint lightly. Dried flowers can also be added if desired. Add a hand-written label with details of fragrance and usage.

Instructions for making **Bath Bombs** are on page 105.

The Soft Option

For snuggly warmth, you just can't beat fur fabric and this crazy duo of hottie cover and cushion are sure to be snapped up, especially by younger buyers. To make the **Cushion**, join two 40cm squares, allowing 1cm seams, turn right side out and stick a contrast fur star (see pattern sheet for outline) on the front. Place a cushion insert inside and close opening (don't bother with zips and buttons).

To make the **Hottie Cover**, cut a 26cm × 70cm rectangle of novelty fur, fold in half crosswise, right sides together and stitch sides, allowing 1cm seams, and leaving a 1cm gap in each side, exactly 4cm from the top edge. Fold under 3cm on top edge and stitch close to inner raw edge, forming

casing (there's no need for a double fold as fur fabric won't fray). Cut two 75cm lengths of cord and thread one half through casing from opening in one side, and the other half from the opposite side. Bind ends of each cord loop together and stitch a 30mm flat button firmly to each end. For toggles, cut two 8cm-diameter circles of fur fabric, run a strong gathering thread around raw edge of each, draw up gathers slightly, stuff firmly with polyester fibrefill, insert button ends of cord into toggle, add a little more stuffing for a nice rounded shape, then pull up tightly around cord and secure firmly (the button prevents cord ends from pulling back out of the toggle when the drawstrings are pulled).

Garden

If you're coordinating a Garden Stall, you need to get your helpers organised well ahead to allow time for seeds to germinate and cuttings to strike. Check out the nurseries in your area for donations of pots, or excess plant stock. When empty pots are donated, make sure they are scrupulously cleaned with soapy water and rinsed, before re-planting. While potted plants are the mainstay of most garden stalls, bunches of fresh flowers and herbs and any other home-grown produce will also sell well. (If donations of flowers are unlikely to be very forthcoming, a pre-dawn trip to your local growers' market can remedy the deficiency for not too much outlay.) Also popular on the stall are tiny potted cacti, grape or ivy prunings twisted into simple dried wreaths, painted terracotta pots of various sizes, decorated gardening gloves, citronella candles (make your own) and gardening aids, such as kneeling pads and aprons with pockets.

Plants & Flowers

Gardener's Hand Balm with lanolin, beeswax & almond oil

Freshly Scented

Bunches of mixed herbs fresh from the garden make delightfully unusual posies that will sell like the proverbial hot cakes, especially at inner city fêtes. Everyone will have different herbs to donate, so request that helpers bring what they can early in the morning of your stall — all varieties of mint, thyme, rosemary, oregano, chillies, lavender, chamomile, feverfew, sprays of bay leaf, sage, lemon balm, basil, scented geraniums, chives, parsley, coriander, lemon verbena and so on — and have volunteers ready to make up the posies. Simply bunch them together decoratively and tie with jute string. Keep them cool in buckets of water and mist them at intervals throughout the day for maximum freshness.

For herbs with short stalks, for an abundance of one particular kind, or simply to add variety to your stall, you can also make up tiny bunches of individual herbs. Modestly priced, they will always sell well, especially if you can add the honest assurance that they are organically grown.

TIP

Encourage those with a surplus crop of lemons to donate them to your garden stall. Not only do they look marvellous sitting on the counter in a big basket, but if you offer them at bargain prices everyone will want a couple.

Spring Tussie Mussies

The variety of small posies that can be assembled for sale is infinite, especially if your fête is in spring or summer. Paper lace doilies and ribbon can add a pretty finishing touch to these old-fashioned nosegays – and don't forget that home-grown natives and lots of interesting (and scented) greenery will also add to the charm of a posy.

Pots of Pleasure

One of the pleasures of a good garden stall is always the interesting variety of plants to be found – usually the result of assiduous gardeners having struck cuttings and raised seedlings some months before the big day. Both methods are relatively easy and involve very little outlay: a large bag of quality potting mix, packets of seeds (unless you're taking cuttings) and small pots. Herbs and chillies will always sell well and look particularly pretty in tiny terracotta pots. So do other small plants, especially if you have timed their growth so that they are flowering on the day of sale – not always possible with every cutting, so don't forget a label with details.

Ivy League

The basis of this ivy heart is a simple wire coathanger bent to shape, with the hook straightened out to insert into the soil. Strands of ivy, willow or other pliant vine, stripped of leaves, are wound around the wire to cover it completely, giving the living ivy a pretty medium around which to grow. A nice finishing touch is the delicate stencilled ivy around the rim of the pot which is echoed in the single stencilled motif on the gardening gloves. The stencil is printed full-size in black on the pattern sheet. Trace it onto stencil film (from craft stores), cut out with a scalpel or sharp craft knife and stencil the design onto pots and gloves as desired, using a paint crayon, fabric paint or artist's acrylic (used sparingly to avoid blobs and leaks). The pots can then be sealed with an exterior quality varnish for extra durability, if desired.

Wearing of the Green

Small children love to add a little water every day and watch the "hair" magically appear on these sprouting heads. Simply encase a few handfuls of potting mix in a tube cut from an old pair of pantihose, forming the mix into a ball with your hands and knotting on each side to form "ears". Before tying the second knot, add a couple of teaspoons of grass seed to the top of the potting mix ball, keeping the seed as neatly as possible in the hair area. Glue on facial features as desired. On your stall, make sure you have a display head that is fully sprouted so that potential buyers can see what will eventually happen to their purchase.

Cook's Treat

Opposite below right: Foodies will enjoys these little muslin pouches filled with dried herbs, known as bouquets garnis. Adding a bouquet garni to a soup, casserole or stock is a traditional way of seasoning and enhancing the flavour of home-cooked dishes.
On a 15cm-diameter circle of muslin or cheesecloth, place 1 teaspoon dried parsley or parsley flakes, 1/4 teaspoon dried thyme leaves and a crumbled bay leaf. Secure tightly with a piece of kitchen twine, leaving a tail to make it easy to remove from the pot. Bouquets garnis can be presented in Cellophane bags, tied with raffia and decorated with sprigs of whole dried herbs, or (opposite below left) in small boxes, decorated with dried bay leaves, a knob of garlic and a raffia bow.

Santa Fe

Small cacti in pots never seem to lose their appeal and are especially popular with children. Buy them wholesale for your stall and plant in brightly decorated tiny terracotta pots for instant success.

Strictly for the Birds

Birdseed bells – very easy and inexpensive to make – add variety to the usual horticultural offerings on your garden stall. Most supermarkets carry birdseed in bulk bags, making it possible to bake several bells in one batch. The egg white used to bind the seed is said to hinder bacterial growth and also has waterproofing qualities, making the bells ideal for hanging outside. They are equally at home, of course, hanging in an aviary or birdcage. Instructions for making them are on page 106.

Earthly Delights

Opposite: For a gardener, a gift box containing a soothing hand balm and protective gloves would make a welcome gift. Enriched with lanolin and vitamin E, the hand cream is decorated with a hand-coloured stamped motif to match the cross stitched design on the gloves. The stamp was also used to decorate a cardboard box for presentation. If adding cross stitch to the gloves seems too labour-intensive, they could also be decorated with the rubber stamp and coloured with fabric pens. Instructions for hand cream and gloves are on page 106.

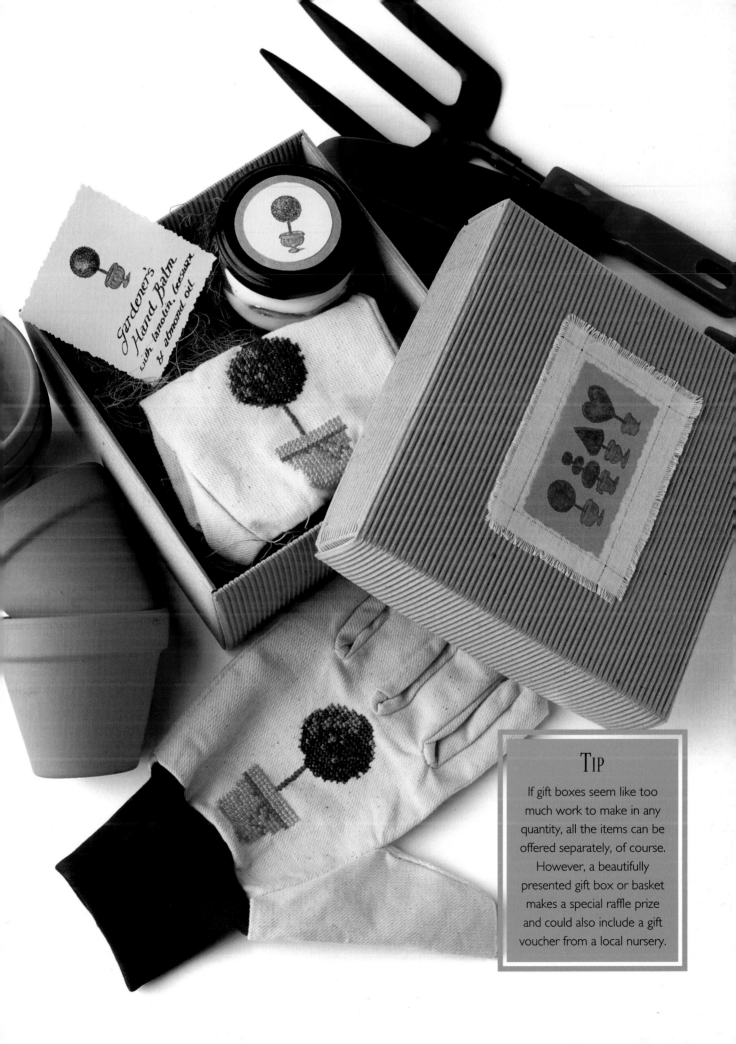

Gardener's
Hand Balm
with lanolin, beeswax
& almond oil

TIP

If gift boxes seem like too
much work to make in any
quantity, all the items can be
offered separately, of course.
However, a beautifully
presented gift box or basket
makes a special raffle prize
and could also include a gift
voucher from a local nursery.

Toys & Kids

Depending on the size of your fair and the space available, you might want to further divide the general category of Toys and Gifts for Kids — by adding a Baby Gifts stall, for instance, by selling Dress-Up costumes separately, or by collecting the things that appeal to teenagers. The main idea, however, is to have lots of items for all the different ages, both things that can be bought **for** children, as well as small inexpensive bits and pieces that can be bought **by** the children themselves — if they've any money left after overdosing at the Sweets Stall! It can also be a good idea to position a face-painter, clown or magician nearby to attract custom. We've included something from all categories in this collection, from babies to young adults, from gifts that will endure, to gimmicks and novelties that will be quite forgotten by the next fête.

Fingertip Fun

Tiny crocheted finger puppet sets will
amuse the littlies for hours as they re-tell
their favourite fairy tales. Use up your
wool scraps for instant best-sellers.
Instructions are on page 107.

King of Beasts

More of a big soft pussycat than a ferocious
beast, this colourful lion puppet is sure to delight
young puppeteers. Easily crocheted from scraps
or inexpensive acrylic yarn, the puppet could
also be easily adapted into a cuddly soft toy.
Instructions are on page 108.

Magic Menagerie

Here's a collection of knitted fantasy creatures that can be knitted up quickly in double yarn, making it easy to have a good supply on hand for those who think a cuddly knitted playmate is the ultimate toy – and they might not all be children! Instructions begin on page 109.

Money Monsters

Endearing, furry monster purses, with their money-hungry mouths and googly eyes, are certain to amuse small children and would make great stocking fillers at Christmas. They require very little in the way of materials and take almost no time to make. Instructions are on page 115.

Lounge Lizard

This friendly fellow will sit plumply in your hand for stroking but can also be trained to lie quite still, keeping a pile of papers under control. Stitched from slithery satin and filled with sand or millet, the lizards are sure to be popular on the craft stall. Instructions are on page 111.

Dressed for Success

Here's a novel idea for a school fête or fund-raiser. Because these delightful dolls take a little bit of time and effort, you're not likely to be making them in great numbers, but a pair of dolls, dressed in your local school uniform would make a wonderful raffle prize. We used mainly second-hand uniforms from the school clothing pool to dress our little pair, so outlay was minimum — but the effect is completely charming. Instructions for both making and dressing dolls begin on page 112.

TIP

The dolls can, of course, be dressed in ordinary outfits as well, and would make very lovable toys.

49

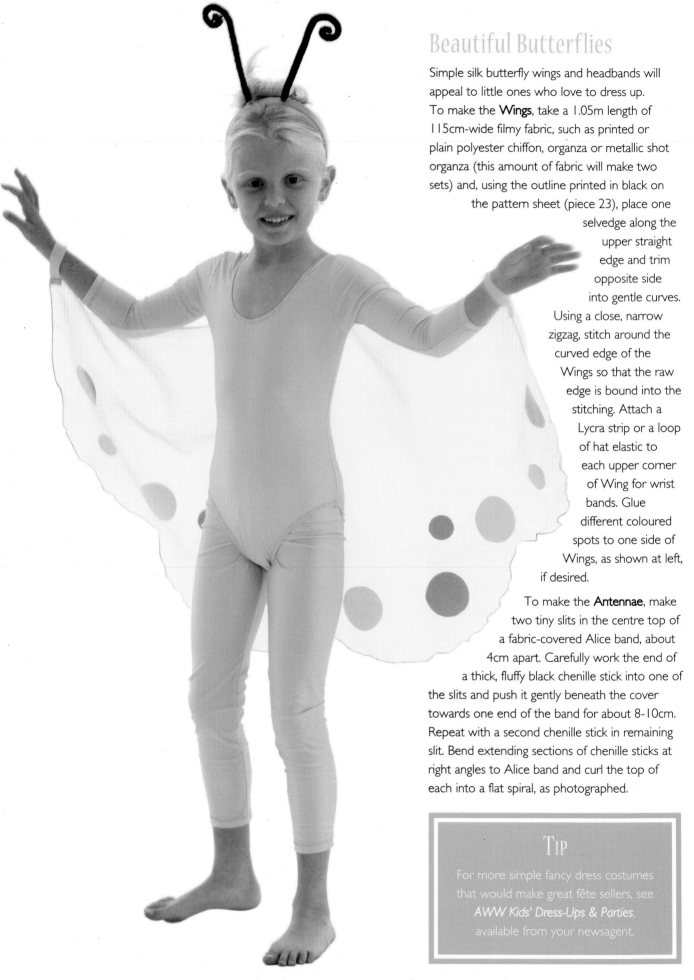

Beautiful Butterflies

Simple silk butterfly wings and headbands will appeal to little ones who love to dress up.

To make the **Wings**, take a 1.05m length of 115cm-wide filmy fabric, such as printed or plain polyester chiffon, organza or metallic shot organza (this amount of fabric will make two sets) and, using the outline printed in black on the pattern sheet (piece 23), place one selvedge along the upper straight edge and trim opposite side into gentle curves. Using a close, narrow zigzag, stitch around the curved edge of the Wings so that the raw edge is bound into the stitching. Attach a Lycra strip or a loop of hat elastic to each upper corner of Wing for wrist bands. Glue different coloured spots to one side of Wings, as shown at left, if desired.

To make the **Antennae**, make two tiny slits in the centre top of a fabric-covered Alice band, about 4cm apart. Carefully work the end of a thick, fluffy black chenille stick into one of the slits and push it gently beneath the cover towards one end of the band for about 8-10cm. Repeat with a second chenille stick in remaining slit. Bend extending sections of chenille sticks at right angles to Alice band and curl the top of each into a flat spiral, as photographed.

TIP

For more simple fancy dress costumes that would make great fête sellers, see *AWW Kids' Dress-Ups & Parties*, available from your newsagent.

Fairy Fantasy

Pretty, glittery wand and tiara sets are must-haves for the fairy folk at your fête. If someone can be persuaded to sew simple tulle fairy skirts as well, you'll make even more dreams come true! To make the **Tiara**, wind 50cm × 0.7mm-diameter galvanised wire around a 4.5cm wide strip of cardboard, as though making a tassel. Loosen wraps slightly and remove wire from cardboard, then twist points gently until you have a line of five equal points. Bend each end of the wire slightly into an L-shape. Cut a length of silver beading wire and twist one end around end of galvanised wire to anchor. Thread beading wire with a pearl or bead, then twist around wire base, then thread with another bead, and so on along the wire, anchoring beads on both sides of the wire. At each of the points as you come to them, thread a teardrop pearl onto beading wire and wind

firmly, so that it stands up on the point. Twist two silver chenille sticks firmly together to create one longer stick, centre beaded wire section on top of a purchased fabric-covered Alice band, then wind chenille stick tightly around both wire and band, starting and finishing at L-shaped ends of wire.

To make a **Fairy Wand**, paint a plain cardboard/dowel wand (from craft stores) with a couple of coats of silver paint. (You could also make the wand yourself from firm cardboard and fine dowelling.) When dry, apply glue to front of star, scatter with silver/blue glitter, dust off excess and allow to dry. Glue a line of pastel or silver sequins around outline of star and add a large faux jewel to the centre.

Something Fishy

A variation on the juggling balls, below, these bouncing bungy-jumping fish look marvellous hanging en masse along the front of a stall. Start by making balls in exactly the same way as the juggling balls. Using craft glue, add joggle eyes and fringed fins and tail cut from balloon scraps. Add a mouth cut from a circular cross-section of a balloon neck, rolled to the desired thickness. The bouncing chain is made from a number of these circular cross-sections looped together to the desired length, then glued to top of fish.

Balancing Act

Colourful juggling balls (package them in sets of three) are very easy to make from balloons and birdseed. Place 100g birdseed into a plastic freezer bag and secure end with a knot. Cut the neck off a round party balloon, leaving just the round part, and insert the seed bag. Cut the neck off another three different coloured balloons, and cut three or four small holes in each round part. Continue to cover the seed ball with these balloons, firming the ball into a nice round shape as you work. The small holes allow the colour underneath to show and appear as spots on the finished ball. Remember, these are definitely not for babies!

Set Expression

Kids will love seeing who can make the ugliest face with these amusingly squishy creatures. Place a cricket ball-sized lump of potter's clay (about 350g) into a plastic freezer bag and knot the top. Place the bag into a large balloon (these are stronger than ordinary party balloons), suck out air so that balloon sits firmly around plastic bag, then knot top firmly. Trim off excess rubber neck and disguise knot with a woollen pompom (see page 119), glued in place for hair. Finally, add joggle eyes and a small purchased pompom nose.

Cover Story

Craft stores and many bargain fabric stores carry a wide variety of wipe-down, colourful vinyl-bonded fabric that is ideal for making children's painting aprons. Cut a 43cm x 60cm rectangle of vinyl and make a pencil mark 7cm in from each side along top edge, and 16.5cm down from corner on each side. Connect marks and cut along lines to shape apron top. For pocket, cut a 21cm x 43cm rectangle of vinyl, turn under 1.5cm on one long edge (top) and topstitch in place. Stitch pocket, right side up, onto lower part of apron, stitching 1cm from side and lower edges. Make two evenly spaced vertical rows of stitching down pocket, dividing it into three equal sections. Turn under and stitch 1.5cm hems on lower edge, straight sides and top of apron (leaving diagonal edges unhemmed). Using the photograph as a guide, stitch 1.5m x 15mm-wide grosgrain ribbon to diagonal sides of apron, allowing a loop of approximately 46cm across neck edge and leaving excess ribbon extending at each side for ties. Stitch close to both edges of ribbon along diagonal edges, for reinforcement.

Spinning Wheels

As old as fairs themselves, traditional paper whirligigs are still as popular as ever with pint-sized customers. If you make them from brightly patterned papers and display them in jars or bottles, they add a vibrant splash of colour to any stall – and you don't need to admit that they cost next to nothing to make! Instructions are on page 114.

The Write Stuff

Young children love small, inexpensive novelty items that they can buy with their own money – this trio of decorated pencils is just the sort of thing (and they'd also make perfect little prizes in a lucky dip). To make the **Pompom Pencils**, right, spread the end of a new pencil with craft glue and wrap a chenille stick up over the end and down around the pencil end in tight coils. Using a glue gun, stick mini-pompoms in place: 25mm for heads and 12mm for ears and muzzles. Add black seed beads for eyes and a dab of paint or embroidered stitches for tip of nose. For the elegant **Jewelled Pencils**, below, thread two or three small beads and a flower-shaped sequin onto a glue-smeared pearl-headed pin. Cover the tip of a new pencil with craft glue and push the extending part of the beaded pin into the tip until the sequin meets the glue. Stick a little ribbon around the top of the pencil beneath the sequin, to finish. And the simplest of all – to make the **Glitter Pencils** (below right), just brush pencils with PVA glue, roll in glitter, shake off excess and allow to dry. Tie several together with metallic organza ribbon, if desired.

54

Bags for Books

All primary school children need a library bag, so they're a great item to sell at school fêtes. Make up a simple 42cm × 33cm (finished size) calico bag with a shoulder strap and stencil it with one of the many attractive stencils available at craft stores. As an added fundraiser at your stall, why not offer to stencil a child's name onto the bag using a fabric pen, while the prospective owner waits?

All Your Marbles

Colourful drawstring bags, filled with marbles or a set of plastic jacks, are cheap and simple to construct from bright craft prints, and are perennially popular with young customers. Our finished bag measures 15cm × 17cm.

Chook Chook!

For a crazy novelty at your fair, try these cackling chooks — people find them irresistible. Knot a longish piece of string firmly through the bottom of any disposable cup and tie a small piece of kitchen cleaning sponge to the other end of the string, which should hang down through the cup. When the sponge is dampened, wrapped around the string and jerked downwards, the cup emits a sound that is extraordinarily like a cackling hen. Add joggle eyes and appropriate features cut from thin coloured cardboard and all day your fair will sound like a poultry yard!

Baubles and Beads

Here are more inexpensive novelty items that will appeal to little girls. The funky **Key Rings**, top left, are cut from two pieces of clear plastic (daisy outline is on pattern sheet in pink). Small novelty buttons or glitter shapes are placed between the plastic daisies and held in place with a circle of stitching. Attach a key ring and chain to finish. To make the cheerful floral **Hair Decorations**, above, simply remove colourful fake flowers from their stems and attach (with stitching or a glue gun) to hair elastics or plain hair clips.

A trip to your local bead shop will provide endless inspiration as well as all you need to make inexpensive **Necklaces**, left. Thread the beads of your choice onto jewellery wire (known as tiger wire) and hold them in place at intervals with tiny crimps that are squeezed together with small pliers. Finish the ends with a loop and hook clasp, and that's it — you'll be amazed at how simple it all is.

To The Lighthouse

This elegant quoits set began life as a collection of timber off-cuts, salvaged from a recycling centre. The main cylinder (about 21cm high and 4cm-diameter) should be very firmly attached to the 20cm x 20cm x 3cm flat base – the best way to do this is to drill a hole into both sections with a large drill bit and glue the pieces together with a dowel joint for reinforcement. The other pieces can be simply glued in place with wood glue. Paint the completed lighthouse and base in colours of your choice, and glue a few stones around the base to simulate a rocky shore. Finally, add the quoits themselves – we used small, inexpensive woven wreaths that we found in a bargain store, but you could also bind lengths of thick rope into rings, or twist other pliable material, such as grape vine or ivy prunings into neat circles.

Toasty Tootsies

Keep little toes warm in a pair of splendid bunny slippers to suit children up to six years. Quickly knitted in garter stitch, the slippers feature contrast ears and a fluffy pompom tail. Instructions are on page 115.

Footy Fever

It seems you can't be too young these days to get into a little team support. These very cute baby "footy bootees", complete with macho "studs", can be knitted in a variety of popular team colours, and we guarantee you won't be able to keep up with the demand! Instructions are on page 115.

Soft Centres

A soft, safe and cuddly gift for a young baby, these colourful balls are very easy to knit in alternating colours or in vibrant stripes. You could also slip a small bell (encased in a tiny plastic container) into the centre of the ball, to make a rattle. Instructions are on page 116.

58

Good Clean Fun

It won't be too much trouble keeping the kids spotless with these colourful novelty bath mitts – they'll *want* to have a bath! Made from simple household sponges, the mitts are quick and very cheap to produce – the ideal fête-make. Instructions are on page 114.

Fuzzy Wuzzies

These zany items are all made from the fabulous array of fun fur fabric now available in craft stores. Choose from dazzling hot colours or a dozen different wild animal prints and watch how popular your stall becomes. For the **Picture Frames** (this page), cut a piece of fur that is several centimetres wider all round than your frame. Place the frame (minus its backing board and glass), right side down, on the wrong side of the fur. Mark and cut away the window area in the centre, taking care to leave a margin of fabric for turning to the back. Clip carefully into each corner of the fabric margins, then fold and glue the fabric around each side of the window to the back of the frame. Do the same with the outside edges, trimming away excess fabric at corners to give a neat, flat finish.

To cover the **Photograph Album** (opposite, centre), simply proceed as though you were covering a school book with paper, gluing excess fabric neatly in place on the inside covers and trimming the fur along the top and bottom of the spine if you can't tuck it down into the spine itself. Add a felt star (trace from pattern sheet), if desired.

The **Shoulder Bag** and **Pencil Case** (opposite) can be made up in a number of different sizes to suit different uses. Instructions for making them begin on page 116.

Christmas

Any fête that occurs in the latter
half of the year can justifiably
feature a Christmas Stall and even
Scrooge will probably find it
enticing, since Christmas seems to
have such universal appeal. Your
Christmas stall could include
handmade cards, gift tags and
wrapping paper (try potato
printing or stencilling), as well as
tree and table decorations, advent
calenders, wreaths, decorative
Christmas stockings and crackers.
To display hand-crafted decorations
to their best advantage and make
your stall look eye-catchingly
festive, set up and decorate a
full-size Christmas tree – if real
ones are unavailable, use an
artificial tree. Fruit cakes and
puddings of various sizes can also
be included on the stall (mini
puddings and gift-wrapped cakes
for one are always popular), but
other traditional Christmas fare,
such as shortbread and mince pies,
would need to be sold within a
week or two of Christmas Day.

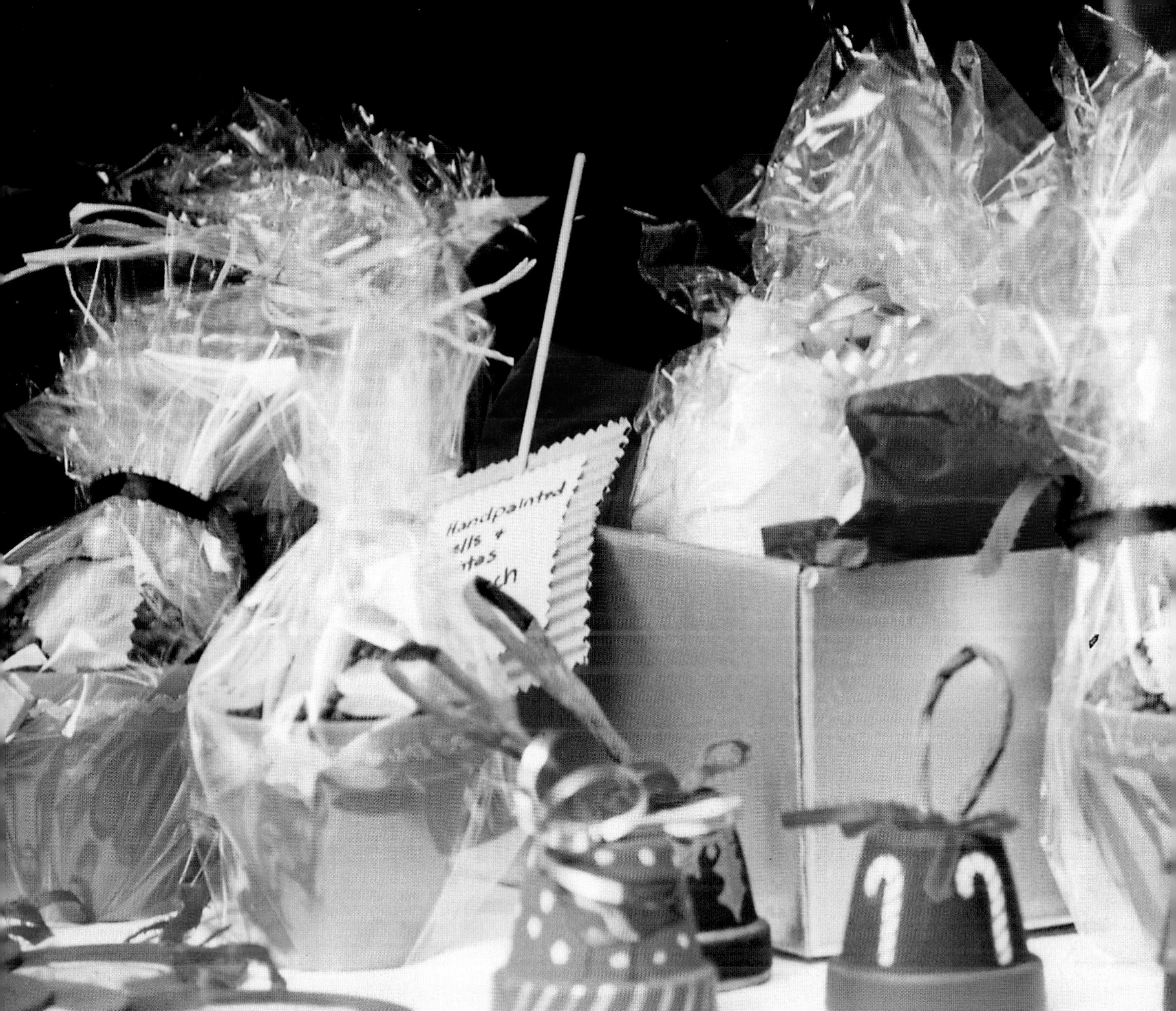
Handpainted

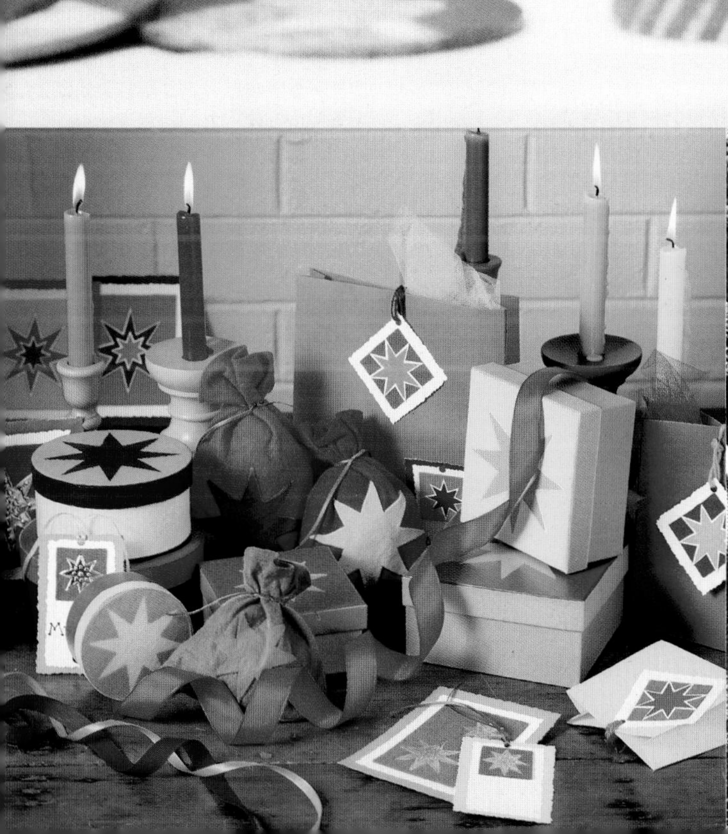

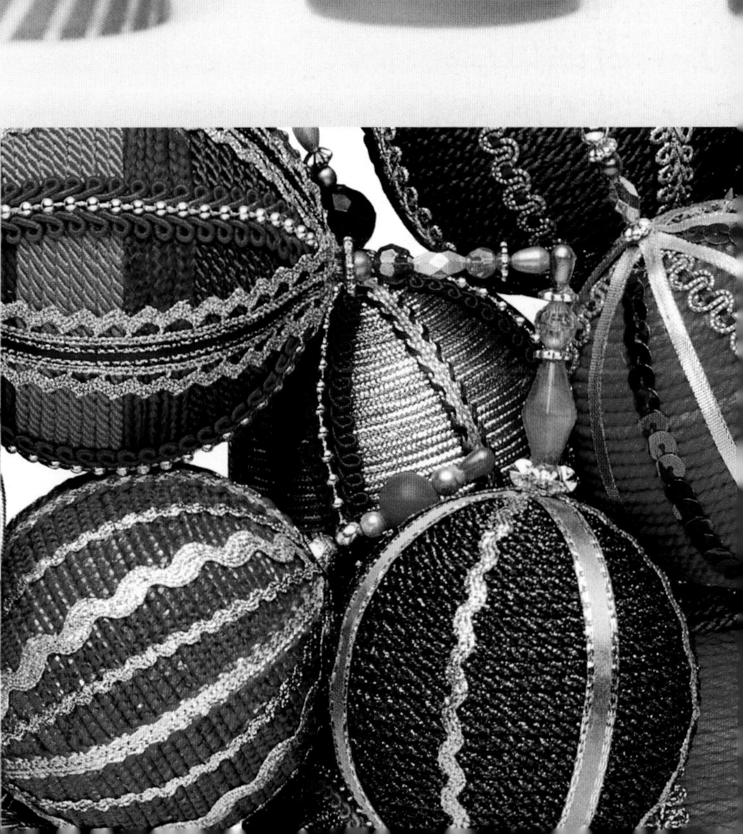

Angels at my Table

No self-respecting Christmas stall would be without a troupe of angels and these charming examples are all very quick and easy to produce. For the rustic **Kitchen Angels**, left, cut and join two calico Head/Body pieces, leaving lower edge open. (Outline, which includes 5mm seam allowance, is printed on the pattern sheet in a grey tone.) Clip curves, turn right side out, stuff firmly and stitch opening closed. Paint upper half with flesh coloured acrylic paint and allow to dry.

Cut a 13cm x 20cm rectangle of fabric and join short edges to form skirt. Run a gathering thread around upper edge of skirt, draw up gathers to fit Head/Body and secure in place. Fray lower edge. Using a glue gun, stick two even-sized bay leaf wings to upper back edge of skirt, then glue a cinnamon stick (or two) below this, for arms. Glue whole star anise to neck edge of skirt, then finish angel with a wisp of doll hair and simple facial features. Glue or stitch a raffia hanging loop to back neck.

For the heavenly blue **Rice Angels**, below, cut and join two triangles of fabric, leaving an opening in one side. (Outline, which includes 5mm seam allowance, is printed on pattern sheet in a grey tone.) Fill with rice and slipstitch opening closed. Push a

little hollow in one point of the rice bag and glue a pink-painted 4cm-diameter polystyrene ball in place for a head. Glue or stitch readymade angel wings to the back (or use the outline on the pattern sheet to make wings from calico and interfacing). Top angel's head with matching mohair or wool, and a brass ring halo. Add a simple face with a black marker pen.

For the quaint **Country Angels** on this page, paint the heads of dolly pegs in a creamy colour, then the rest of the peg in colours to match simple gathered skirts made from fabric scraps. Cut corrugated cardboard wings (outline is on pattern sheet in pink), paint in the same colour as the face and glue to back of peg. Finish each angel with twig arms, a little doll hair, a hanging loop and facial features, applied with a fine black marker – don't forget to add a little blush to the cheeks.

65

Deck the Halls

As purchasers remove the decorations they want to buy from your display Christmas tree, extras can be added from a supply beneath the counter.

Pearly Stars, below, are very easy to make and can be decorated with small pearls or beads in any colour scheme you choose (op-shops are a great source of cheap pearls and beads). Wrap 0.7mm galvanised wire 11 times around a 4.5cm-wide piece of heavy cardboard, as though making a tassel (width of cardboard determines the length of the star points and can be varied). Loosen wraps slightly and remove from cardboard, then twist points into a star shape, overlap ends and twist together. Cut a length of silver beading wire (or fine fuse wire) and twist one end around wire star to anchor. Thread beading wire with a pearl, twist around star wire a couple of times, thread with another pearl, and so on around star until you reach starting point again. Wrap wire thread tightly around star to finish and trim end with pliers. Add a hanging loop.

All that is required for the beautiful **Sequin Baubles**, right, is a little patience – they can be as simple or elaborate as you wish, and could also be made by older children. The easiest to make are those where sequins, in one or several colours, are pinned to the surface of a polystyrene ball (short 16mm craft pins give the best results), overlapping slightly until ball is completely covered.

For fancier designs, lightly pencil outlines onto the ball before starting. To finish balls, add metallic ribbon, small beads, contrast sequins, pearl-headed pins or, to highlight a colour change, outline the border with a string of tiny pearls or silver beads, using extra pins to keep it in place. Add decorative hanging loops.

Braid-Wrapped Balls, opposite, take a little more time but are really not difficult to make and can be sold for a great deal more than they actually cost to produce. Spread one half of a 6-7cm polystyrene ball with PVA glue. Starting at the top, wind fine braid, crochet cotton or other thread around the ball in a spiral, keeping threads closely butted to each other. Stop when you get to the centre of the ball, and leave excess thread hanging. Spread remaining half of ball with glue and repeat process, starting at the opposite pole and working towards the centre as before – this method allows you to adjust any unevenness at the centre, then cover the adjustment with a broader ribbon if need be. Trim excess thread at centre points. Glue decorative ribbon and braid around ball as desired, and decorate with small beads, sequins, pearl-headed pins and bits of cheap costume jewellery, as photographed. Attach a hanging loop to the top with a pin and sequin.

TIP

Buy cheap undyed cotton
cord by the reel or metre
and dye it yourself.

Partridges in Pear Trees

OK, so they're not pear trees and the birds aren't much like partridges either – but they certainly *smell* like Christmas! Fragrant with the spicy aroma of cloves, the "pear tree" is actually an old-fashioned pomander, used since Elizabethan times to scent a room or cupboard. With the addition of colourful little felt birds masquerading as partridges, these potted pomanders make attractive and unusual folk decorations for a Christmas table or mantelpiece. Instructions for making are on page 118.

TIP

Pomanders can also be presented in the traditional way – in small organza or voile drawstring bags, or tied with a decorative ribbon for hanging in cupboards.

A Pig in a Poke

Ham Bags are always great fête favourites – inexpensive to make from stencilled calico and infinitely preferable to an ancient pillowcase for storing the Christmas ham! Instructions are on page 117.

68

Baby's First Christmas

Irresistibly cute, Santa Bibs for baby's
first Christmas dinner will be a
drawcard for new parents and proud
grandparents. They could be teamed
with simple Santa hats if you desire.
Instructions are on page 117.

South of the Border

Christmas decorating doesn't have to be all holly and ivy. Rustic embossed **Tinfoil Stars** are a traditional part of Mexican folk art and the hot, bright colours of the felt outlines add instant cheer to a Christmas decorating scheme. Using the star shapes printed in various sizes on the pattern sheet in black, trace star outlines onto thin aluminium shim (available from craft stores) or even onto the bottoms of disposable aluminium baking trays, using a stylus or dry ballpoint pen, and working on an old magazine for padding. Emboss a simple design within the star shape, using the photograph as a guide, then cut out star, leaving a narrow border beyond the embossed outline. Cut a piece of silver cord for a hanging loop and glue the ends under one point of the star. Glue the star to a piece of felt, then cut felt to star shape, leaving a narrow border all round. Once you've mastered stars, try other simple shapes such as hearts, birds, fish and angels. The embossed shapes can also be glued to coloured cardboard Christmas cards and gift tags – always good sellers.

We also used the star shapes to make decorative matching tags for a collection of colourful gift bags of various sizes. To make the **Gift Bags**, using the diagram on the pattern sheet and adjusting the measurements as desired, cut bag shape from thin cardboard or heavy paper. On the wrong side, score along marked lines. Fold top flap and side tab to inside along score lines. Use double-sided tape (less messy than glue) to secure side tab in place on inside of opposite side edge. Before closing base flaps, fold inverted pleats in side edges along score lines. Fold in side base flaps, then front and back base flaps and secure with double-sided tape. Base of bag can be reinforced with a cardboard insert if desired. Punch holes in upper edge of bags for attaching handles or tags.

To make **Gift Tags**, trace star outlines on the pattern sheet onto coloured paper and cut out. Glue stars to contrast paper and cut out again, leaving a narrow contrast border. Next, glue each star to a coloured felt or paper background square and mount this on a deckle-edged tag. Deckle-edged scissors, available inexpensively from craft and specialist paper stores, are a quick way to give your work a professional finish. Punch a hole in the corner of each tag and attach to Gift Bags with coloured cord or ribbon.

70

Off the Peg

Old fashioned dolly pegs feature in these delightful traditional tree decorations. For the **Victorian Soldier**, right, paint the lower half of a peg black and the upper half scarlet, leaving the "head" unpainted.

From oven-bake modelling clay (such as Fimo) make a simple black hat (a 1.5cm cylinder to fit head of peg, with a semi-circular brim), a black moustache and straight scarlet arms. Pierce hat from top to bottom with a skewer, then bake pieces according to manufacturer's instructions. When cool, thread a hanging loop through hole in hat and glue hat to head with craft glue so that ends of loop are secured. Glue remaining pieces in place, then paint details with yellow paint, as photographed.

To make **Santa Claus** or **Saint Nicholas**, at right, drill a hole through each dolly peg at shoulder level, using a narrow bit. Paint pegs in Christmas red (for Santa Claus) or burgundy (for Saint Nicholas), adding black "boots" and flesh-coloured heads. Push a white or pink chenille stick through the drilled hole and trim to size for arms. Wrap a strip of thin quilt wadding around body for padding, securing end with glue. Using the coat pattern (printed on the pattern sheet in black), cut a coat from red or burgundy felt – short for Santa Claus and long for Saint Nicholas. Lapping front seams over back, glue seams together with craft glue (or stitch if preferred). Use narrow strips of quilt wadding to trim coats as photographed. Place coat onto peg body and glue centre front closed. Add a black felt belt with painted gold buckle. Glue hair, beard and moustache (made from quilt wadding or polyester rovings) in place. Cut a hat or hood from felt scraps and glue to head, folding, trimming and gluing as necessary to fit head. Add eyes with black marker pen, and a hanging loop to finish.

These colourful blonde **Angels** are the easiest of all. Using glitter paint, draw a "leotard" onto peg body and allow to dry. Cut a 15cm length of 5cm-wide wired ribbon, remove wire from one edge, run a gathering thread around edge, pull up gathers to fit angel's waist, tie off, then glue skirt around waist. Using a glue gun, glue a hanging loop to back of peg, then glue two nylon-covered wired petal "wings" (available in bunches from craft stores; cut off their wire stems if necessary) over the loop ends and decorate wings with glitter paint if desired. Add a little curly hair and a simple face.

71

Get Cracking

Easy and fun to make, Christmas crackers can be fanciful, traditional, elegant, rustic – indeed, any style you please, as you can see from our gorgeous examples. Sell them individually or wrapped in Cellophane in sets of six. Snaps (the bits that go bang) can be bought in bundles from craft shops.

From thin cardboard, cut one rectangle, 10cm × 17cm, for inner tube, and two rectangles, each 4.5cm × 17cm, for outer ends. Roll each piece of cardboard into a cylinder, overlapping 1.5cm, and secure with sticky tape. Using deckle-edged scissors or pinking shears, from coloured tissue or crêpe paper, cut a rectangle, 36cm × 18cm. From contrast paper, cut a rectangle, 33cm × 18cm. (If using crêpe paper, make sure the grainline runs along the cracker, not around it.) Place smaller rectangle on a flat surface, wrong side up, and centre larger rectangle on top so that equal amounts overlap at each end. Position inner tube in centre of paper, then place a smaller tube at each end, with about 5cm in between. Secure tubes to paper with a little double-sided tape.

Make simple paper hats from tissue paper, using your own head for size. Insert folded paper hat, small gift, short joke (get ideas from kids' joke books) and snap into inner tube, securing snap with a little double-sided tape. Roll paper layers around tubes and secure with double-sided tape. Gently squeeze crackers between tubes and tie with raffia or ribbon, as tightly but as gently as possible. The outer tubes keep the ends of the cracker in a nicely rounded shape. Decorate finished crackers as desired.

Food

The irresistible lure of homemade goodies spells instant financial success for a community fair — and the wider the variety of goods on offer, the greater this success will be. A clever way to ensure you have lots of stock for a school cake stall is to buy cake boxes in wholesale quantities, get every child to decorate one, then send the decorated boxes home with the request that they be returned on fair day filled with something yummy. To maximise sales, you should also sell single slices and biscuits as well as whole cakes, and position a couple of chairs and tables beneath a market umbrella to serve morning and afternoon teas. Of course, cakes and sweets are only part of the story — get the jam and pickle makers organised well beforehand (set up a jar collection centre to provide enough empty containers) and encourage anyone with a gourmet specialty to provide a delicious sample or two for your "Gourmet Gifts" section.

TIP

Cakes can also be topped with coloured sprinkles, chopped nuts or toasted coconut. Icing can be tinted with a few drops of food colouring, or flavoured with grated citrus rind or sifted cocoa.

Cup Cakes

125g butter
1 teaspoon vanilla essence
²/₃ cup (150g) caster sugar
2 eggs
1¹/₃ cups (200g) self-raising flour
¹/₄ cup (60ml) milk
200g packet Smarties

VIENNA CREAM
125g butter, softened
1¹/₂ cups (215g) icing sugar mixture
2 tablespoons milk

Cream butter, essence and sugar, add eggs one at a time, beating well after each addition. Stir in sifted flour and milk alternately, beat until smooth. Place paper patty cases into patty tins. Drop teaspoonfuls of mixture into each patty case. Bake in moderate oven (180°C/350°F) 15 to 20 minutes. Cool on wire rack.

When cold, spread top with Vienna Cream, decorate with Smarties in a daisy pattern.

Vienna Cream: Place butter in small bowl of electric mixer, beat until butter is as white as possible, gradually add about half the sifted icing sugar, beating constantly. Add milk gradually, then gradually beat in the remaining icing sugar.

Makes 24 cakes.

Un-iced cakes suitable to freeze for up to 1 month.

Toffees

Can be made up to 3 days ahead; store in an airtight container.

3 cups (660g) sugar
1 cup (250ml) water
¹/₄ cup (60ml) brown malt vinegar
coloured sprinkles, if desired

Line muffin pans with paper patty cases; spray patty cases with cooking oil spray, if desired, to prevent toffee sticking to paper.

Combine sugar, water and vinegar in medium saucepan; stir over low heat until sugar is completely dissolved.

Bring to boil; boil rapidly, uncovered, about 15 minutes or until a small amount of syrup will set when spooned into a glass of cold water, or when a sugar thermometer reaches the "crack" stage (154°C). Remove pan from heat, allow bubbles to subside. Carefully pour syrup into prepared pans. Stand toffees 2 minutes before decorating with sprinkles.

Makes about 15.

Not suitable to freeze.

Toffee Apples

For the sticks, you can use disposable wooden chopsticks available in pull-apart pairs from Asian food stores. Toffee apples may be made up to 2 days ahead; store in an airtight container but do not refrigerate.

10 wooden sticks or skewers
10 small green or red apples
4 cups (880g) caster sugar
1 cup (250ml) water
¹/₃ cup (80ml) glucose syrup
¹/₂ teaspoon red or green
   food colouring

Cover two oven trays with baking paper and set aside.

Push a wooden skewer or stick three-quarters of the way through each apple from stem end. Wash apples under cold water, stand on a cake rack until completely dry (do not rub apples with a cloth).

Combine sugar, water, glucose and colouring in a large saucepan, stir over low heat until sugar is dissolved.

Bring sugar mixture to a boil, then boil, uncovered, for about 10 minutes, or until a few drops of mixture snap, crackle and immediately harden when placed in iced water (or until mixture reaches 154°C on a sugar thermometer). Remove from heat and allow bubbles to subside.

Tilt pan slightly to one side to give a deep pool of toffee. Carefully dip a skewered apple into toffee, twist slowly to coat apple completely; remove apple slowly (air bubbles will form in the toffee if apples are dipped too fast).

Twirl apple around a few times over pan, place on prepared tray. Repeat with remaining apples. Leave to set at room temperature. Wrap in Cellophane if desired.

Makes 10 toffee apples.

Not suitable to freeze.

Twice-Baked Biscuits

This simple recipe makes "120 biscuits", which is their alternative name. Baking biscuits twice allows them to remain crisp for longer. Can be made up to 1 week ahead; store in an airtight container.

500g margarine or butter, softened
1 cup (220g) caster sugar
400g can sweetened condensed milk
5 cups (750g) self-raising flour
1½ tablespoons finely grated lemon rind
½ cup (100g) finely chopped glacé ginger

Beat margarine or butter and sugar in large bowl with electric mixer until smooth. Add condensed milk, flour, lemon rind and ginger in batches; beat until combined.

Roll heaped teaspoons of mixture into balls, place balls onto lightly greased oven trays, about 4cm apart; flatten lightly with a fork. Bake in moderate oven (180°C/350°F) about 10 minutes or until light golden brown; cool biscuits on trays.

Biscuits can be arranged closer together on trays for second baking as they will not spread any further. Bake cooled biscuits in moderate oven (180°C/350°F) about 8 minutes or until golden brown; cool biscuits on trays.

Suitable to freeze.

TIP

Tie biscuits together with ribbon or raffia. Use dry lasagne pasta for labels and write on labels with a permanent marker.

Choc-Chip and Peanut Biscuits

Crushed nuts are packaged chopped peanuts. Biscuits can be made up to 1 week ahead; store in an airtight container.

250g butter, softened
2 teaspoons vanilla essence
2 cups (400g) firmly packed
brown sugar
2 eggs
3½ cups (525g) self-raising flour
250g packet Choc Bits or
Milk Bits
1 cup (140g) crushed nuts

Beat butter, essence and sugar in small bowl with electric mixer until smooth, add eggs, beat until well combined. Add sifted flour, Choc Bits and nuts, press ingredients together using hands. Divide mixture into 2 portions, roll each portion into two 40cm logs. Roll each log in baking paper or foil, refrigerate for at least 1 hour or overnight.

Cut logs into 1cm slices with serrated knife. Place slices on baking paper-lined trays, about 3cm apart.

Bake in moderate oven (180°C/350°F) about 20 minutes or until browned lightly; cool biscuits on trays.

Makes about 80.

Logs suitable to freeze.

Coconut Macaroons

Macaroons can be made up to 1 week ahead; store in an airtight container.

2 egg whites
1/2 cup (110g) caster sugar
1 teaspoon vanilla essence
2 tablespoons plain flour
1 1/2 cups (135g)
   desiccated coconut

Beat egg whites and sugar in small bowl with electric mixer about 10 minutes or until sugar is dissolved. Stir in essence, sifted flour and coconut in 2 batches. Line oven trays with baking paper. Drop level tablespoons of mixture onto trays, 5cm apart. Bake in slow oven (150°C/300°F) about 40 minutes or until lightly browned; cool on trays.

Makes about 25.

Suitable to freeze.

Rocky Road

Crushed nuts are packaged chopped peanuts. Rocky Road can be made up to week ahead; store in an airtight container in the refrigerator.

375g milk chocolate Melts
30g Copha, chopped
1/3 cup (45g) crushed nuts
2 tablespoons desiccated coconut
2 x 250g packets pink and
   white marshmallows

Lightly grease 20cm x 30cm lamington pan, line base and sides with foil. Combine chocolate and Copha in heatproof bowl, stir over pan of simmering water until smooth; remove from heat. Spread 1/3 cup (80ml) of chocolate mixture over the base of prepared pan, immediately sprinkle with nuts and coconut, then marshmallows.

Drizzle evenly with remaining chocolate mixture, gently tap pan on bench to settle chocolate. Refrigerate until set. Cut into pieces.

Not suitable to freeze.

Almond and Sesame Brittle

Almond kernels are unblanched almonds. Brittle can be made up to 1 week ahead; store in an airtight container.

- **2 cups (440g) sugar**
- **1/4 teaspoon cream of tartar**
- **1/2 cup (125ml) water**
- **2 tablespoons golden syrup**
- **60g butter**
- **1 1/4 cups (200g) almond kernels, toasted**
- **1/3 cup (50g) sesame seeds, toasted**
- **1/2 teaspoon bicarbonate of soda**

Lightly oil 26cm x 32cm Swiss roll pan. Combine sugar, cream of tartar and water in medium pan, stir over low heat until sugar is dissolved. Brush side of pan with pastry brush that has been dipped in hot water to dissolve any sugar crystals. Bring to boil; boil uncovered, for about 7 minutes or until the mixture turns golden brown.

Remove pan from heat, stir in golden syrup and butter, return pan to heat, boil further 1 minute.

Remove pan from heat, add nuts, sesame seeds and soda, stir until well combined. Pour mixture into prepared pan; cool. When cold, break into pieces.

Not suitable to freeze.

Fudge-Frosted Chocolate Cake

This cake stays fresh for at least 3 days. Store in an airtight container. Cut into smaller pieces for sale.

2 cups (500ml) water
3 cups (660g) caster sugar
250g butter, chopped
1/2 cup (50g) cocoa powder
1 teaspoon bicarbonate of soda
3 cups (450g) self-raising flour
4 eggs, beaten lightly
1 tablespoon vanilla essence

FUDGE FROSTING
90g butter, chopped
1/3 cup (80ml) water
1/2 cup (110g) caster sugar
1 1/2 cups (240g) icing
 sugar mixture
1/3 cup (35g) cocoa powder

Grease two 20cm x 30cm lamington pans, line bases with baking paper.

Combine water, sugar, butter, cocoa and soda in pan; stir over low heat until sugar dissolves. Boil, then immediately simmer, uncovered, for 3 minutes.

Transfer mixture to large bowl; cool. Gradually add sifted flour, eggs and essence; beat with electric mixer until smooth. Pour mixture evenly into prepared pans. Bake in moderate oven (180°C/350°F) about 35 minutes. Stand cakes 10 minutes before turning onto wire racks to cool. Spread cold cakes with a layer of Fudge Frosting.

Fudge Frosting: Combine butter, water and sugar in small pan; stir over heat until sugar is dissolved. Sift icing sugar and cocoa into bowl; stir in hot butter mixture, in batches. Cover, refrigerate 1 hour or until frosting is thickened. Beat until spreadable.

Un-iced cakes suitable to freeze.

Old-fashioned Honeycomb

This delicious, crunchy sweet has nothing to do with real honeycomb made by bees, but has been popular with generations of Australian children. It may be made up to 3 days ahead and stored in a airtight container.

1 1/2 cups (330g) sugar
1/3 cup (115g) golden syrup
1/3 cup (115g) honey
1/3 cup (80ml) water
2 teaspoons bicarbonate of soda

Line base and sides of a 28cm × 18cm rectangular slice pan with baking paper.

Combine sugar, golden syrup, honey and water in a large saucepan and, using a wooden spoon, stir constantly over low heat until sugar is dissolved. Bring to a boil; reduce heat, simmer for 12-15 minutes or until a small amount becomes hard when dropped into cold water (154°C or hard crack stage on a sugar thermometer). Mixture burns easily so take care at this stage.

Remove pan from heat; using a wooden spoon, quickly beat in finely-sifted soda (mixture will foam up in the pan). Spread immediately into prepared tin but do not handle too much as the honeycomb will deflate. Allow to cool 30-45 minutes or until completely cold. Remove from tin, break into pieces.

Suitable to freeze but may be a little sticky when thawed.

TIP

Honeycomb pieces may be dipped in chocolate (melt 180g dark or milk chocolate with 185g Copha) and placed on baking paper until set. Store in an airtight container in the refrigerator.

Caramel Peanut Popcorn

Can be made up to 1 week ahead; store in an airtight container.

1 tablespoon vegetable oil
1/3 cup (70g) popping corn
3/4 cup (110g) unsalted peanuts, toasted
250g butter
1 1/2 cups (330g) sugar
1/3 cup (115g) honey

Lightly oil 26cm x 32cm Swiss roll pan, line base and sides with foil, brush foil with a little oil.

Heat measured oil in large pan, add popping corn, cook, covered, over medium heat, shaking pan occasionally until popping stops.

Transfer popcorn to prepared Swiss roll pan; discard any corn that has not popped. Sprinkle peanuts over popcorn.

Combine butter, sugar and honey in medium pan, stir over low heat until sugar is dissolved. Bring to boil; boil uncovered, about 4 minutes or until rich golden brown. Pour caramel mixture over popcorn. Stand about 15 minutes before cutting into squares.

Not suitable to freeze.

Popcorn suitable to microwave.

> ### TIP
> Popcorn can also be presented in paper cups.

Caramels

400g can sweetened condensed milk
1 cup (220g) caster sugar
125g butter
1/2 cup (175g) golden syrup

Place all ingredients in a medium saucepan, stir over low heat until sugar is thoroughly dissolved. Bring to a boil; boil, stirring constantly. Continue stirring 8-10 minutes, or until desired colour: the darker the colour, the harder the caramel.

When desired colour, remove from heat, allow bubbles to settle; pour into oiled and lined 20cm square tin. Do not scrape pan (put scrapings back into another tin, as this may "candy").

When cold, cut into pieces with an oiled knife.

Not suitable to freeze.

Marshmallows

60g gelatine
1 cup (250ml) cold water
1kg (4¹/₂ cups) sugar
1¹/₂ cups (375ml) water, extra
2 teaspoons vanilla essence
2 teaspoons lemon juice

Line a 23cm slab pan with baking paper.

Soften gelatine in cold water. Place sugar and extra water in a large saucepan, stir over low heat to dissolve sugar. Bring to a boil, stir in soaked gelatine, boil, uncovered, for 20 minutes. Remove from heat and allow to cool to lukewarm. Add essence and lemon juice.

Beat until very thick and white. Pour into prepared pan. Allow to set. Cut into squares, roll in icing sugar or toasted coconut.

To toast coconut: Place coconut in heavy pan, stir with a wooden spoon over moderate heat until coconut is light golden brown. Remove from pan immediately or coconut will continue to cook in heat of pan.

Not suitable to freeze.

Coconut Ice

Coconut ice can be made up to 1 week ahead and stored, covered, in the refrigerator.

5¹/₄ cups (760g) icing
** sugar mixture**
2¹/₂ cups (225g) desiccated
** coconut**
400g can sweetened
** condensed milk**
1 egg white, lightly beaten
pink food colouring

Line a deep 19cm square cake pan with foil.

Sift icing sugar into large bowl, stir in coconut, then milk and egg white; stir until well combined.

Press half the mixture into prepared pan. Tint remaining mixture pink, press evenly over first layer; cover, refrigerate several hours before cutting into squares.

Not suitable to freeze.

Daisy Biscuits

These pretty biscuits may be made up to 5 days ahead; store in an airtight container.

125g butter
1 teaspoon vanilla essence
²/3 cup (150g) caster sugar
1 teaspoon grated lemon rind
2 eggs, lightly beaten
2 teaspoons milk
1 ¹/3 (200g) cups
  self-raising flour
1 cup (150g) plain flour
6cm daisy cutter

ICING
2 egg whites
3 cups (480g) icing sugar
  mixture
yellow food colouring
piping bag with fine point
thin cardboard

Beat butter, sugar and essence in small bowl with electric mixer until smooth. Add grated lemon rind, eggs and milk, beat until just combined. Stir in sifted flours; mix to soft dough. Knead on lightly floured surface until smooth. Cover, refrigerate 30 minutes. Roll dough between sheets of baking paper until 5mm thick. Cut out shapes using daisy cutter, place on lightly oiled oven trays and bake in moderate oven (180°C/350°F) about 10 minutes or until firm. Cool on wire racks.

Icing: To make a stencil for daisy centre, trace around daisy cutter onto thin cardboard and cut out. Remove a circle from the centre (tracing around a coin makes this easier).

Beat egg whites until soft peaks form. Gradually stir in sifted icing sugar mixture. Tint a small portion of mixture with yellow food colouring, leaving the remainder white.

Place cardboard stencil over biscuit and, using a knife, smooth yellow icing over centre hole. Lift stencil cleanly away, leaving biscuit with a round yellow centre. Repeat for remaining biscuits, wiping stencil with paper towel as necessary.

Spoon white icing into piping bag fitted with a small plain tube. Outline each biscuit with a fine white line, and allow to set.

Not suitable to freeze.

Banana Bugs

These boggle-eyed chaps are always a hit with littlies. They can be prepared up to 2 weeks ahead.

banana sweets
Minties, or other
  wrapped sweets
Jaffas, or other round sweets
Cellophane
sticky tape
30cm coloured chenille sticks

Place two banana sweets, one Mintie and two Jaffas along the centre of a small Cellophane strip, fold in sides and ends of Cellophane, forming a wrapped packet and secure underneath with sticky tape. Cut a chenille stick in half, twist one half around the packet between the Jaffas and Mintie; twist the second half around the packet between the Mintie and bananas, creating body sections of bug. Bend ends of chenille sticks into "legs" underneath, as photographed.

Not suitable to freeze.

Baby Bunting Biscuits

Another novelty treat for small children, these biscuits can be prepared 2 days ahead and stored in an airtight container. The Cake Mate remains soft, so store in single layers, taking care not to smudge faces.

2 egg whites
3 cups (480g) icing sugar
  mixture
250g packet Milk Arrowroot
  biscuits
Cake Mate Decorating Gel in
  colours as desired
Smarties
coloured paper napkins
small white sticky labels
fine gold or silver marking pen

Beat egg whites in medium bowl until soft peaks form. Gradually stir in sifted icing sugar mixture.

Using a flat blade knife, spread icing over rounded side of biscuits. Place on wire rack, stand, uncovered, at room temperature, until set.

Decorate biscuits using Cake Mate to draw faces and a "kiss curl". Use a Smartie to represent a dummy. Wrap biscuits in paper napkins in the shape of a baby's nappy; secure nappy with a paper sticker on which you have drawn a simple safety pin in gold or silver.

Makes 33 Baby Bunting biscuits.

Not suitable to freeze.

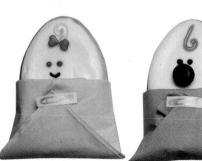
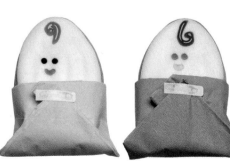

TIP

If you don't have a piping set, roll a piece of baking paper into a tight cone and snip off the tip to make a simple piping bag. The finished biscuits may be presented in decorated papier mâché boxes or wrapped in Cellophane.

Three Fruits Marmalade

Marmalade may be made up to 12 months ahead provided it is properly bottled and sealed. Store in a cool dark place.

- **4 large (880g) oranges**
- **2 medium (360g) lemons**
- **1 medium (390g) grapefruit**
- **1.25 litres (5 cups) water**
- **1.5kg (6 cups) sugar, approximately**

Cut unpeeled fruit in half, cut halves into thin slices. Remove seeds, tie in piece of muslin. Combine fruit, muslin bag and water in non-metal bowl, cover, stand overnight.

Transfer mixture to large saucepan, bring to a boil and simmer, covered, about 1 hour or until rind is soft. Discard muslin bag.

Measure fruit mixture and return to pan. Add 3/4 cup sugar for each cup of fruit mixture. Stir over heat without boiling, until sugar is dissolved. Bring to a boil, boil uncovered, without stirring, for about 40 minutes or until marmalade jells when tested. Stand for 10 minutes, then pour into hot, sterilised jars, filling right to the top; seal while hot.

Makes about 7 cups.

Not suitable to freeze.

TIP

Both marmalade and citrus butters look particularly attractive when presented in stencilled jam covers or with a stencilled tag. Trace an appropriate section of the design at left onto stencil film and cut out with a scalpel, remembering that you need a separate stencil for each colour. Stencil the designs onto tags or calico circles, using a sparing amount of paint. Stitch narrow ribbon to the edge of the circles to finish, or use pinking shears.

TIP

A tangy Lemon Butter can be made by substituting extra lemon juice and rind for the orange juice and rind. A combination of lime and lemon is also delicious.

Citrus Butter

Citrus butter can be made up to 1 month ahead and stored in the refrigerator. For selling, add a tag that says "Keep refrigerated".

4 eggs
3/4 cup (165g) sugar
1 teaspoon finely grated lemon rind
1/4 cup (60ml) lemon juice
1 teaspoon finely grated orange rind
1/4 cup (60ml) orange juice
1/4 cup (60ml) water
125g unsalted butter, chopped

Whisk eggs and sugar together in a large microwave-safe bowl; gently stir in the remaining ingredients.

Cook butter mixture, uncovered, in a microwave oven on MEDIUM (55%) 6 minutes, whisking every 2 minutes.

Cook mixture, uncovered, on MEDIUM (55%) about 2 minutes or until it thickens, whisking once during cooking. Pour into hot sterilised jars; seal while hot.

Makes about 2 cups (500ml).

Not suitable to freeze

Flavoured Vinegars

These flavoured vinegars are best made at least 1 week ahead, and may be made up to 3 months ahead. Store in a cool dark place.

Herb and Garlic Vinegar

1 litre (4 cups) white wine vinegar
8 sprigs fresh tarragon
2 cloves garlic, peeled, sliced

Peppered Rosemary Vinegar

1 litre (4 cups) white wine vinegar
10 black peppercorns
10 sprigs fresh rosemary

Berry Cardamom Vinegar

1 litre (4 cups) white wine vinegar
300g raspberries
10 cardamom pods, crushed

Wash fresh herbs or berries and pat dry before using. Combine all the ingredients for your chosen vinegar in large jug or bowl; cover tightly and refrigerate for 3 days. Pour the vinegar (strained if you wish) into dry sterilised bottles; seal tightly.

Fresh herbs can be added just before fair day, but they too will discolour with time.

Makes about 1 litre (4 cups) each vinegar.

Not suitable to freeze.

TIP

Ask friends to save their small, decorative bottles for you. If they come without lids, add a tight-fitting cork and seal with sealing wax, which looks lovely. Add tiny handwritten tags detailing the ingredients and perhaps a possible use. Decorate the tags with whole spices, or a dried sprig of the main herb used to flavour the vinegar.

Barbecue Sauce

Barbecue Sauce can be made up to 2 weeks ahead; store in refrigerator. For selling, write "Keep refrigerated" on labels.

2 tablespoons vegetable oil
2 medium (300g) brown onions, chopped finely
3 cloves garlic, crushed
1/2 cup (125ml) treacle or firmly packed brown sugar
1/3 cup (90g) Dijon mustard
1/3 cup (80ml) Worcestershire sauce
800g can tomatoes
1/2 cup (120g) tomato paste
1 cup (250ml) water
1 tablespoon cornflour
2 tablespoons water, extra

Heat oil in pan; cook onions, stirring, until very soft. Add garlic, treacle, mustard, sauce, undrained tomatoes, paste and water; simmer, uncovered, stirring occasionally, about 20 minutes or until thick. Stir in combined cornflour and extra water; simmer, stirring, until thickened. Blend or process sauce until smooth; push through sieve. Pour sauce into hot sterilised jars; seal while hot.

Makes about 1.5 litres (6 cups).

Suitable to freeze.

Tomato and Choko Chutney

Chutney can be made up to 3 months ahead; store in refrigerator. For selling, write "Keep refrigerated" on labels.

2 x 800g cans diced tomatoes
2 large chokos, peeled, cored, chopped finely
2 medium (300g) onions, chopped
1 1/2 cups (375ml) malt vinegar
2 cups (400g) firmly packed brown sugar
2 tablespoons mustard powder
1 tablespoon mild curry paste or powder
2 cloves garlic, crushed
1 teaspoon ground allspice
2 teaspoons coarse cooking salt
1/4 teaspoon ground black pepper
1 tablespoon cornflour
1/4 cup (60ml) malt vinegar, extra

Combine undrained tomatoes, chokos, onions, vinegar, sugar, half the mustard powder, curry paste, garlic, allspice, salt and pepper in large pan. Stir over heat, without boiling, until sugar is dissolved. Simmer uncovered, stirring occasionally, about 1 1/2 hours or until thickened. Combine remaining mustard powder, cornflour and extra vinegar in small bowl; stir until smooth. Gradually stir cornflour mixture into chutney; simmer, stirring, about 5 minutes or until thick. Pour into hot sterilised jars; seal while hot.

Makes about 2.25 litres (9 cups).

Not suitable to freeze.

TIP
Use recycled, sterilised, unchipped bottles. Add a tiny cloth or hessian "hat" to cover any existing labelling on the lid, and tie with raffia or jute string. Pop-sticks also make novel labels — glue a chilli to one end.

Old-Fashioned Lemon Cordial

Mixture may be made up to 2 weeks ahead; store in the refrigerator.

3¹/₂ cups (750g) sugar
15g citric acid
7.5g tartaric acid
1.9 litres (7¹/₂ cups) water
juice of 4 lemons
grated rind of 2 lemons

Combine sugar, citric and tartaric acid in a large bowl. Bring water to a boil and pour it over the sugar, citric and tartaric acid, stir until sugar is dissolved. Add lemon juice and rind, allow to cool. Pour into sterilised bottles and seal with corks or screw tops.

To drink, dilute with iced water or soda water.

TIP

Sell bottles of undiluted cordial by all means, but an old-fashioned lemonade stall will also draw plenty of customers, especially on a hot day. Invest in lots of ice, dilute the cordial with water or soda water and serve with slices of lemon and sprigs of fresh mint or lemon balm.

Instructions

Tomato Pincushion

Page 15

Measurements

Approximately 8-9cm diameter.

Materials

- 30cm x 20cm red fabric (felt, velvet, red prints, and so on)
- Scrap of green felt for calyx (felt or fabric)
- Red or green embroidery thread
- Polyester fibrefill
- Small amount double-sided interfacing

Pattern pieces

Both pattern pieces are printed on pattern sheet in a pink tone. Trace Tomato and Calyx.

Cutting

NOTE. Seam allowance has not been added to Tomato outline. If you are using felt, you don't need to add allowance, as segments are oversewn together close to the edges. However, if you are mass-producing and want to use the sewing machine, even for felt, then add 5mm seam allowance to all edges. If you are using woven fabric, you should also add 5mm seam allowance around all edges (or more if your fabric frays badly). Do not add allowance to the Calyx outline.

From red fabric or felt, cut four Tomatoes, on the bias, adding seam allowance if appropriate.

If using green felt, cut one Calyx outline. If using green fabric, fuse two scraps together with double-sided interfacing, then cut one Calyx outline. (This provides a stiffer fabric and prevents the edges from fraying.)

Method

1 TOMATO With right sides together, stitch Tomato segments together around curved edges, leaving straight edge open. Turn right side out. Fold under seam allowance on top edge (if added) and run a gathering thread around edge. Fill tomato firmly with fibrefill, then pull up gathering thread. Tie off securely.

Using a long length of embroidery thread (full number of strands; use two threads together if your thread is fine), anchor end at top point of tomato, then take thread around tomato to bottom point, up though centre of tomato and around again, as before. Work around tomato in this manner, dividing it into segments, by running thread along seam lines and down the middle of each section (eight segments in all). Pull thread slightly as you work, creating characteristic dimples in top and bottom. Tie off thread securely.

2 CALYX & STALK Stitch Calyx in place over gathers at top of tomato, then make a stalk by rolling a scrap of fabric into a tight cylinder and stitch in place at centre top.

Terracotta Candle Pots

Page 18

Measurements

Our pots are 8cm diameter x 7cm high; design can be adapted to fit any size pot.

Materials

- Small terracotta pots
- Masking tape
- Clear acrylic sealer

- Chalk pencil
- Artist's acrylic paints: Warm White and Dark Blue
- Brushes: No 6 flat and No 0 liner
- Candles to fit pots

Method

1 PREPARATION Wash terracotta in detergent and water with a scouring pad to remove any dirt and grease. Allow to dry.

Place a strip of masking tape along lower edge of rim. Using No 6 flat brush, basecoat rim with two coats of Warm White mixed with an equal amount of clear sealer. Carefully remove masking tape and allow paint to dry.

Use chalk pencil to draw zigzag cross-hatching on rim, using diagram below as a guide.

2 ADDING PATTERN Mix Dark Blue paint with an equal amount of clear sealer and paint cross-hatching, using No 0 liner brush. Leave to cure a few days before use.

Padded Coathangers

Page 20

Measurements

Finished hanger is approximately 42cm long.

Materials

- Wooden coathanger with screw-in hook
- Essential oil, such as lavender (optional)
- 0.2m x 150cm polyester wadding
- 20cm-wide fabric strip, about twice the length of hanger (see **NOTE**, below)
- 4cm x 20cm bias strip of fabric, to match or contrast
- 6mm-wide satin ribbon, for trim

NOTE. A pretty border effect can also be achieved by using two contrast fabrics for front and back of cover. In this case you need one 8.5cm-wide strip (front) and one 12.5cm-wide strip (back), each twice x length of hanger.

Method

1 ADDING SCENT If you are using essential oil, remove hook from hanger and rub oil into wood to delicately scent finished hanger.

2 WADDING Cut two strips of wadding, each approximately 5cm wide x 80cm long (shorter strips can be joined if necessary). Butt one short end of each strip together and join them with long stitches that do not pucker the wadding. Screw hook into coathanger.

Wind wadding strip firmly and evenly around hanger from one end to other, then back again. Stitch end of wadding in place to hold.

Place padded coathanger on its side onto remaining wadding and trace outline of hanger to make a snug-fitting extra cover for the padded hanger. Cut two pieces of wadding to your traced size and stitch these around the coathanger, butting edges neatly.

3 COVER Fold fabric cover strip in half lengthwise, right sides together; slightly round corners at each end. Stitch one short edge and long edge with a 5mm seam, leaving a tiny hole in centre of long seam for hook. Turn cover right side out and press.

(If you are using two contrasting fabrics, stitch them together along both long edges, allowing 5mm seams and leaving a tiny hole in centre of one seam for hook. Turn right side out and press so that an equal amount of contrast border appears at both top and bottom of cover. Slightly round corners at each end, then turn wrong side out again and stitch one end. Turn right side out and press again.)

Using a long machine stitch, run a line of gathering along each long edge, about 1cm from edge, leaving excess thread trailing at each end. To allow for hook, at centre point on top edge, raise presser foot and move fabric to reinsert needle about 5mm from stopping point.

Remove hook from hanger and carefully insert padded hanger into cover. Fold in raw ends and slipstitch opening closed. Before pulling up threads, centre the opening in top edge and screw hook firmly back into place.

Working from both ends, pull up gathering threads until cover fits snugly onto padded hanger. Tie off threads securely and bury ends.

4 HOOK Fold bias strip in half lengthwise, right sides together and edges matching. Stitch 6-7mm from fold, then stitch again 7-8mm from fold. Cut off excess fabric close to second row of stitching. Turn bias right side out (using a loop turner or a needle and double thread to pull it through), then slide cover over hook. Tuck top raw end inside and hand-stitch end to secure. Pull cover firmly down over hook, trim away excess length and tuck lower raw end down into cover of hanger. Secure with a couple of hand-stitches.

5 FINISHING Tie satin ribbon around hook and tie in a bow at the front.

Decorated Evening Bags

Page 21

Measurements

Finished bags measure approximately 17cm x 25cm, but measurements can be adapted to make smaller or larger bags.

Materials

- 38cm x 19cm satin, brocade, silk dupion, or other evening fabric
- 66cm x 19cm contrast fabric for lining and border
- 0.6m twisted satin cord or braid
- Scraps of brocade, braid, tassels, beads, jewels and so on

Method

1 BAG With right sides together and allowing 1cm seams, stitch short ends of Bag rectangle and lining rectangle together. Press seams open.

With right sides together, fold bag/lining so that seams are exactly aligned with each other; pin. Stitch both side seams as pinned, leaving an opening in one side of lining for turning. Turn right side out through opening; slipstitch opening closed. Push lining down into bag, wrong sides together. Edge of lining will protrude above bag, forming contrast border. Press.

2 DECORATION This is entirely up to you. Handles can be made from the same fabric as bag or from satin cord. Border can be decorated with braid, ribbon or beading, as desired. Add tassels, toggles, decorative buttons, jewels, lace – whatever you have in your store of pretty bits and pieces.

Découpaged Pillboxes

Page 22

Measurements

Boxes range from 4cm to 5.5cm in diameter.

Materials

- Craftwood pillboxes, available from craft stores (you could also use small papier mâché boxes if you can't find craftwood)
- Sandpaper
- All-purpose water-based sealer
- Pictures from wrapping paper or old calendars
- Tracing paper
- Curved nail scissors or découpage scissors
- Gloss spray sealer
- Artist's acrylic paint in colours to coordinate with pictures
- Metallic gold acrylic paint
- Assorted brushes and small sponge
- PVA glue and Clag paste
- Vinegar
- Fine metallic gold cord, optional
- 450 adhesive (if using cord)
- Water-based gloss varnish

Method

1 PREPARATION Sand and seal boxes, both inside and out.

Trace shape of each box lid onto tracing paper and cut out. Use this translucent "frame" to help choose an image for découpage, placing it over selected images to make sure they will fit within circle of lid. When you've selected a picture, place box lid over picture and trace around it. Cut out just inside drawn line – use nail scissors with the curve pointing inwards in order to achieve a perfect circle.

Seal picture front and back with gloss spray sealer. Place picture on box lid to make sure it fits exactly – any overhang must be trimmed off.

2 BASECOAT & PAINTING Using a colour that coordinates with your chosen picture, paint outside of box and lid. Use a single colour or sponge several shades over entire surface. If sponging, dip sponge into paint, remove excess on paper towel, then dab sponge over the dry basecoat colour. You don't need to rinse the sponge between colours.

Paint inside of box and lid, as well as rims and base with metallic gold paint. Allow to dry. Gold dots around lid rim can be added, if desired, using wrong end of a paintbrush. To paint a ring of tiny roses, use a small liner brush.

3 DÉCOUPAGE Mix equal parts of PVA glue and Clag paste, and glue sealed picture to lid. Press out any excess glue and wipe away with a damp cloth. Allow glue to dry.

Mix a little vinegar in water and, using a damp cloth, wipe this over box to remove any traces of glue or grease. If you wish to add metallic gold cord trim, glue this around rim with 450 adhesive before varnishing.

4 VARNISHING Finish with several coats of water-based gloss varnish. You might find it convenient to stand box upside down on a cardboard toilet roll while varnish is drying. You don't have to sand between coats or apply the usual 20 coats of varnish, as these boxes are

varnish, you can lightly sand the box and re-coat, wiping away all traces of dust before doing so. If you are mass-producing, you might also consider using one of the thicker, one-coat glass-finish varnishes, available in craft stores.

Silk Strawberries

Strawberries, actual size

Measurements

About 4cm long (the size of real strawberries).

Materials

◆ Silk dupion scraps (15cm will make 10 strawberries)
◆ Matching thread
◆ Polyester fibrefill or dried lavender
◆ DMC gold embroidery thread (Art 282)
◆ Gold seed beads (we used Mill Hill Gold 00557)
◆ 0.3m x 6mm-wide satin or silk ribbon (per strawberry), in desired colour for calyx
◆ Gold cording yarn (such as Twilley's Goldfingering or Coats' Aurora)
◆ Gold pebble beads (we used Mill Hill Gold 05557)
◆ Clear craft glue

Method

1 STRAWBERRY Trace pattern for the Strawberry, which is printed on the pattern sheet in a pink tone. Cut one Strawberry piece from silk fabric, placing straight side of pattern piece on the grain running *across* silk width.

Fold Strawberry in half, right sides together, and stitch along straight side, allowing a 7mm seam. Turn right side out.

Using double thread, work running stitch around open edge, turning seam allowance under as you go. Pull up thread a little and stuff strawberry with fibrefill or lavender, then pull up fully and secure.

2 GOLD THREAD Using gold thread and ⋯⋯⋯ form a decorative grid over ⋯⋯⋯ in diagrams.
⋯⋯⋯ erry, work running stitch along ⋯⋯ point, then back to ⋯⋯⋯ opposite s⋯ e (**Diagram 1**).
Using fabri⋯⋯ ⋯ake a second line of running stitc⋯⋯ **Diagram 2**.
Follow grain line for eac⋯ ⋯sive line of stitches, keeping lines approxim⋯ ly 1cm apart.
Finally, work lines of run⋯ ing stitch across the grain, forming a grid of squares (**Diagram 3**).

3 GOLD BEADS Stitch a gold seed bead to the middle of each square, using matching polyester thread and a back stitch.

4 CALYX With satin or silk ribbon, make a calyx by creating six overlapping loops, each in a figure-of-eight formation. Secure

loops to each other with a few tiny stitches in the middle. Trim ends of the ribbon neatly.

5 CORD Make a cord by twisting approximately 80cm of gold yarn tightly, then folding in half so that the threads twist around each other. Knot free ends to prevent unravelling. Fold cord in half and, with a few small stitches, secure both ends of gold cord to top of ribbon calyx. Thread a gold pebble bead onto cord and knot to hold in place.

6 FINISHING Carefully glue completed calyx to top of strawberry.

Diagram 1

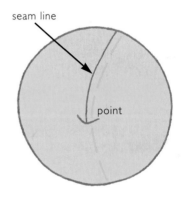

Diagram 2

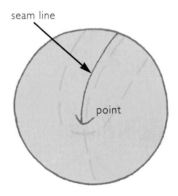

Diagram 3

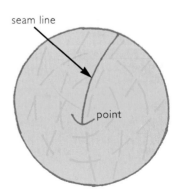

Love Birds

Page 24

Measurements

Approximately 6cm high, excluding crest.

Materials (per bird)

◆ Two 9cm squares luxury woven fabric, such as brocade, figured satin, watered taffeta, and so on
◆ Sequins and tiny seed beads
◆ Coloured feathers
◆ 2cm square felt, for beak
◆ Polyester fibrefill or rice, for filling

Method

1 PREPARATION Overcast edges of fabric squares to prevent fraying.

2 EYE On right side of each square, stitch a sequin and bead eye in the corner, positioning it 12mm in from the edges.

3 BEAK Cut felt square diagonally in half, giving two Beaks and reserve one Beak for another bird. Baste remaining Beak to right side of one fabric square, point inwards, with top corner level with top of eye.

4 CREST Position crest feather/s at corner of one square, on the right side, and hold in place with a couple of basting stitches.

5 JOINING SQUARES Place squares right sides together, aligning eyes and, allowing 4mm seams, stitch top edge, front edge and lower edge, sandwiching feather crest and Beak, and leaving a 4cm opening in centre of lower seam for turning. Leave seam opposite Beak unstitched.

6 TAIL Arrange three tail feathers and tuck inside body cavity through open tail seam, placing quill end of feathers in the centre of the seam, aligned with the top and lower seams.

Stitch seam through all layers, forming a "pyramid" shape and sandwiching tail at the same time. Turn bird right side out through opening in lower seam, pushing out corners.

7 FILLING Fill birds with the stuffing of your choice – fibrefill should be firmly packed; the heavier filling requires slightly less. Slipstitch opening closed.

Log Cabin Lorikeet/Galah

Page 24

Measurements

Birds sit about 7-9cm high.

Materials

NOTE. This method makes two identical birds. See **Diagram 1**, opposite, for colour choice.

◆ 7.5cm square fabric in Colour A, for centre square
◆ 2.5cm × 112cm strips of fabric in Colours A, B, C, D and E (following **Diagram 1** for colour choice)
◆ Two 25cm × 6cm strips Colour D (or 25cm × 6cm strip in each of Colours D and B, for Lorikeet)
◆ Scrap of grey (Galah) or red (Lorikeet) felt
◆ Black (Galah) or red (Lorikeet) embroidery thread, or red and black seed beads
◆ 25cm × 6cm thin wadding
◆ Polyester fibrefill, rice or teddy "beads", for filling

Pattern pieces

Pattern pieces are printed on pattern sheet in black. Trace Beak and Lorikeet Tail or Galah Tail onto thin cardboard for templates.

Cutting

NOTE. Pattern pieces and given measurements **include** 6mm seam allowance, unless otherwise indicated.

From felt, cut two Beaks in black (Galah), or red (Lorikeet).

Place wadding strip on work surface, top with a Colour D rectangle, right side up, then top that with another Colour D rectangle (Galah), or a Colour B rectangle (Lorikeet), wrong side up. Trace appropriate Tail shape twice onto the wrong side of the uppermost fabric (you are making two complete tails), but do not cut out. Pin layers together to hold.

Method

NOTE. All seams are stitched with right sides together, with a 6mm seam allowance. Do not trim each strip to correct length until after it is stitched in place – this saves both time and fabric.

1 PATCHWORK Stitch a Colour B strip to opposite sides of centre square A, press seam allowances towards strip, then trim top and bottom edges even with square. (For Lorikeet only, trim 5mm from long edge of each B strip, as lime green should feature as a narrower band of colour on finished bird's neck.)

Stitch a Colour C strip to top and bottom of square, press and trim as before. Following **Diagram 1**, proceed in this manner, adding colours as designated, until square is complete.

2 EYE Using red (Lorikeet), or black (Galah) embroidery thread, work French knots (see **Embroidery Stitch Guide** on page 119) in each corner of centre square, 1.5cm in from seam lines. Alternatively, stitch a red or black seed bead in each corner, if preferred.

3 CUTTING PATCHWORK Measuring accurately, cut patchwork square exactly in half, following cutting line shown on **Diagram 1**.

4 TAIL Following traced outline, stitch around edge of Tail "sandwich" through all layers, leaving straight edge open. Repeat for second outline. Trim away excess fabric around outlines, clip curves and turn tails right side out, sandwiching wadding between fabric layers. Press lightly. Transfer markings to tails with a light pencil or chalk pencil and topstitch along markings. To avoid messy thread ends, start sewing from open end, pivot on needle at end of tail and stitch back on the same line. Thread ends can then be concealed in the seam.

5 ASSEMBLY With right sides together and straight raw edges even, baste Beak (facing inwards) to raw edge of corner square, placing lower corner of Beak on seam line between corner square A and strip C.

Following fold line on **Diagram 1**, fold patchwork in half crosswise to form a square, matching seam lines exactly. Starting at "head"

Diagram I

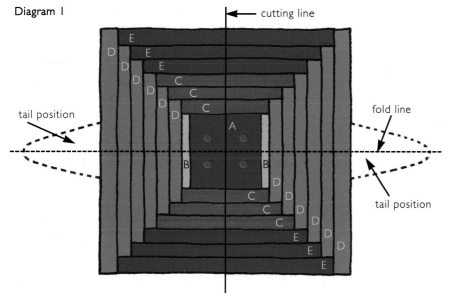

cutting line

tail position

fold line

tail position

LORIKEET
A = Royal blue
B = Lime green (¹/₂ width)
C = Red
D = Bright green
E = Royal blue

GALAH
A = White
B = Pink (full width)
C = Pink
D = Grey
E = Pink
● = eye

(corner square), stitch front seam, sandwiching Beak, then stitch lower seam, leaving a gap of about 4cm in lower seam for turning. Leave seam opposite Beak unstitched. (When the bird is folded into its "pyramid" shape, this will be the tail seam.)

Place tail, tip-first, through open tail seam into body cavity, with Colour B underside (Lorikeet only) facing lower seam of block, matching centre point of tail to both lower seam and centre fold line (**Diagram I**), raw edges even. Stitch seam through all layers, forming a "pyramid" shape and sandwiching tail at same time. Turn bird right side out through opening in lower seam, pushing out corners.

6 FILLING Fill birds with the stuffing of your choice – fibrefill should be firmly packed; the heavier filling requires slightly less. Slipstitch opening closed.

Log Cabin Cockatoo
Page 24

Measurements

Birds sit about 7-9cm high.

Materials (per bird)

◆ Two 4cm white squares, for centres
◆ Assortment of 2.5cm-wide white and off-white fabric strips: damask, white-on-white pattern, different textures and so on
◆ 2.5cm square black felt for Beak
◆ Lemon yellow feathers or 4cm square lemon yellow felt for Crest
◆ 10cm square each white and pale yellow fabric, for Tail
◆ 10cm square thin wadding
◆ Black embroidery thread or black seed beads
◆ Polyester fibrefill, rice or teddy "beads", for filling

Pattern pieces

Pattern pieces are printed on pattern sheet in black. Trace Beak, Cockatoo Tail and Cockatoo Crest (if using felt instead of feathers).

Cutting

NOTE. Pattern pieces and given measurements **include** 6mm seam allowance, unless otherwise indicated.

From black felt, cut one Beak.

From yellow felt, cut one Crest (if you are not using feathers).

Place wadding square on work surface, top with pale yellow square, right side up; top that with white square, wrong side up. Trace Tail shape onto wrong side of uppermost fabric, but do not cut out. Pin layers together to hold.

Method

NOTE. All seams are stitched with right sides together, with a 6mm seam allowance. Do not trim each strip to correct length until after it is stitched in place – this saves both time and fabric.

1 PATCHWORK With raw edges even and allowing a 6mm seam, stitch a 2.5cm strip to one side of centre square. Cut off excess strip in line with edge of square (see **Diagram 2**) and press seam allowances towards strip.

Diagram 2

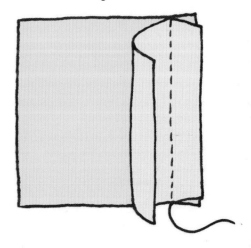

Turn patch so that completed strip is at top of square and sew second strip of different fabric to next side of centre square. Trim end of strip even with square, as before (**Diagram 3**). Press seam allowances towards strip.

Diagram 3

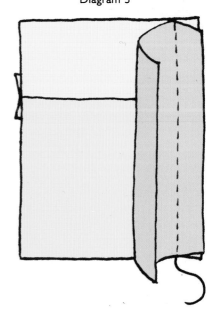

Continue sewing strips onto sides, changing to a different fabric each time until there are three rows of strips on each side (**Diagram 4**). If you don't have 12 different fabrics, repeat those already used, keeping selection random.

Diagram 4

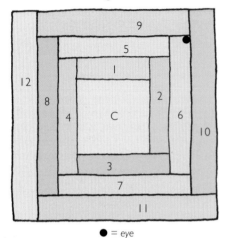

● = eye

Complete a second log cabin square in the same way – squares do not need to be identical as long as you use the same range of fabrics.

2 TAIL Complete Tail as for Lorikeet/Galah, **Step 4**, on page 98.

3 EYE Attach a seed bead or work a French knot (see **Embroidery Stitch Guide** on page 119) for each eye at upper corner of each block, just inside last round of strips, as indicated on **Diagram 4**.

4 BEAK Baste Beak (facing inwards) to right side of block, with straight edge of Beak aligned with straight edge of block and top of Beak approximately level with eye.

5 CREST Baste Crest or feathers to right side of top edge of block, with front edge of Crest approximately level with eye.

6 ASSEMBLY Place remaining block on top, right sides together and eyes aligned. Stitch along top edge, front edge and lower edge, sandwiching Crest and Beak at the same time and leaving a 4cm opening in lower seam for turning. Leave seam opposite Beak unstitched. (When the bird is folded into its "pyramid" shape, this will be the tail seam.)

Place tail, tip-first, through open tail seam into body cavity, with pale yellow underside facing lower seam of block, matching centre point of tail to both lower seam and top seam, raw edges even. Stitch seam through all layers, forming a "pyramid" shape and sandwiching tail at same time. Turn bird right side out through opening in lower seam, pushing out corners.

7 FILLING Fill bird with the stuffing of your choice – fibrefill should be firmly packed; the heavier filling requires slightly less. Slipstitch opening closed.

Log Cabin Potholder

Page 25

Measurements

20cm square.

Materials

- ◆ Small amount red cotton fabric
- ◆ Small amounts cotton fabric, in six dark colours and six light colours
- ◆ 0.3m x 90cm coordinating cotton fabric, for backing
- ◆ 20cm square thin polyester wadding
- ◆ Quilting thread
- ◆ Quilting needle

Cutting

NOTE. All given measurements **include** 5mm seam allowance.

From red fabric, cut one 4cm square, for centre.

Cut remaining fabrics (except backing) into 2.5cm-wide strips, the longest of which will need to be approximately 20cm in length.

Method

NOTE. All seams are stitched with right sides together, with a 5mm seam allowance. Do not trim each strip to correct length until after it is stitched in place – this saves both time and fabric.

1 PATCHWORK With raw edges even and allowing a 5mm seam, stitch a light-coloured strip to one side of red centre square, then trim end of strip even with square (see **Diagram 2**, on page 99). Press seam allowance towards strip.

Turn patch so that completed strip is at top of square. Stitch a second light-coloured strip to centre square and first strip. Trim end of strip even with square (see **Diagram 3**, page 99). Press seam allowance towards strip.

Stitch a dark-coloured strip to the next edge of the centre square in the same way, then press and trim, as before.

Stitch another dark strip to the remaining side of the square, then press and trim.

Continue stitching strips in this manner, following the order in **Diagram 4** and using the photograph as a guide to placing light and dark strips. Continue until there are five rows of strips on each side.

2 BACKING Cut a square of backing fabric 1cm larger all round than the patchwork. Centre patchwork on backing, wrong sides together, with wadding sandwiched in between. Baste layers together or use pins to keep layers firmly sandwiched.

3 QUILTING Using quilting thread and needle, stitch a row of small quilting or running stitch (see **Embroidery Stitch Guide** on page 119) around centre square about 3mm in from seam line, taking care to stitch through all layers. Quilt around each row of strips in the same way. Remove basting. (If mass producing, quilting can be done by machine, but will not look as rustic.)

4 BINDING Trim excess wadding only. Turn under 5mm on all edges of backing fabric. Bring folded edge of backing over raw edge of patchwork to form a false binding. Pin in place.

5 HANGING LOOP Cut a 10cm x 2cm strip of backing fabric, fold in half lengthwise, right sides together. Stitch 5mm from edge, trim and turn right side out. Pin ends under binding at one corner, stitch securely. Slipstitch binding in place around potholder (or stitch by machine, if preferred).

Patchwork Glasses Case

Page 24

Measurements

Approximately 11cm x 19cm.

Materials

NOTE. The following amounts will make about 10 cases. If mass-producing, make up a large piece of strip-piecing and cut to required size.

◆ Assorted, coordinating strips of cotton fabric, 50cm long and varying widths, from 2-4cm

◆ 0.5m × 115cm cotton print, for lining

◆ 0.5m × 115cm thin polyester wadding

◆ 8m purchased or homemade bias binding, in coordinating colour

Method

1 STRIP-PIECING Pin wadding to wrong side of lining, working from the centre to outside edges and keeping lining smooth.

Pin first fabric strip, right side up, onto non-lined side of wadding, starting on the 50cm left edge and making sure that pins are close to the left edge of strip. Place a second fabric strip right side down on top of first strip, and pin into place, just enough to hold strips together.

Using a straight machine stitch and aligning the right outer edge of the presser foot with the right edges of the two layers of fabric, stitch through all layers. At all times, be careful not to hit the pins securing the wadding and lining, and remove them as you sew to avoid trapping them between the layers.

Flip the second strip over to be right side up and flatten the seam with your fingers. Lay a third strip on top, right sides together and raw edges even, and stitch as before.

Continue until all the wadding is covered with strips, taking care to keep them straight and parallel with the edges. The top layer may have a tendency to "creep", but the extra allowance in the bottom layers will compensate for this.

2 MAKING UP CASE When strip-piecing is complete, cut the fabric "sandwich" into 45cm × 10cm pieces.

Using 11cm lengths of bias binding, make a flap-stay for each case by folding each strip in half lengthwise and stitching edges together by hand or machine. Set stays aside.

Bias bind one narrow end of the quilted strip and trim the corners of the other end into a neat curve (**Diagram 1**).

Baste ends of flap-stay to right side of fabric, 5cm below bound end. The stay is slightly longer than the width of the quilted strip to allow for the flap to tuck under it.

Bringing wrong sides together, fold the lower end of case 18cm up towards the top (**Diagram 2**). Open out bias binding, fold the raw end under about 5mm and, with right side of binding to right side of case, and starting at the crosswise fold of case, stitch binding to case through all layers, securing ends of flap-stay at the same time. Stop stitching about 3cm from

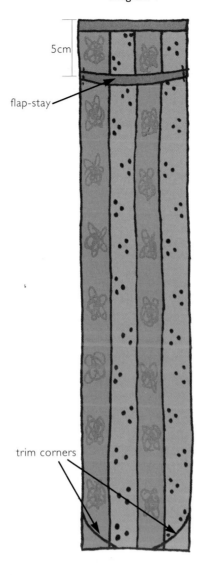

Diagram 1

5cm

flap-stay

trim corners

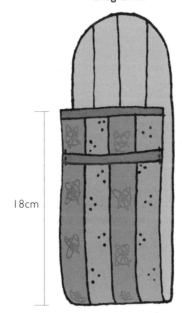

Diagram 2

18cm

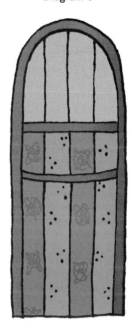

Diagram 3

the end and, leaving needle in the fabric, cut off excess bias, leaving it extending by about 5mm. Fold under this extension and continue stitching to the end of the case (**Diagram 3**).

Trim seam, turn binding to other side and slipstitch in place, neatening across ends as well.

The Bag Bag

Page 29

Measurements

42cm x 20cm.

Materials

◆ 0.5m × 112cm calico or homespun (enough for two Bags)

◆ Stencil film, such as Mylar

◆ Fine black marker pen

◆ Scalpel or craft knife

- Self-healing cutting board
- Artist's acrylic paint in chosen colour
- Fabric or textile medium
- Stencil brush
- 0.6m × 6mm-wide elastic

Method

1 PREPARATION Pre-wash, dry and press fabric. For each Bag, cut one rectangle, 46cm x 42cm, and one strip, 3.5cm x 30cm, for hanging loop.

2 CUTTING STENCIL Stencil design is printed full size in pink on pattern sheet. Using black marker pen, trace design onto stencil film, then cut out carefully with a scalpel or craft knife.

3 APPLYING STENCIL Mix fabric medium and paint according to manufacturer's instructions. Centre stencil on Bag rectangle. Dip brush in paint, dab off extra onto paper towels, then apply paint to stencil using a sharp, short dabbing motion, up and down over design until stencil is completely covered. It is important to keep brush almost dry to prevent paint seeping under stencil and spoiling the design. If you need more paint, always dab off excess before applying the paint to the stencil.

When stencilling is complete, lift stencil cleanly away and allow fabric to dry completely. When dry, press on the reverse with a hot iron to set the paint.

4 MAKING UP BAG Fold stencilled rectangle in half lengthwise, right sides together, and stitch centre back seam, allowing a 1cm seam. Neaten seam with zigzag or overlocking.

Press under 5mm around top edge, then press under another 1.5cm. Stitch close to both pressed edges to form casing, leaving a small opening for threading elastic. Stitch a similar casing on lower edge.

5 HANGING LOOP Fold hanging loop in half lengthwise, right sides together. Stitch long edges, turn right side out, fold in ends and topstitch close to all edges. Pin ends of loop to top edge of bag on each side of centre back seam, then stitch in place along top and bottom casing lines.

6 FINISHING Cut elastic into two equal pieces and thread through casings at top and bottom of bag. Stitch ends of elastic to secure and slipstitch openings closed.

Mushroom Bag

Page 29

Measurements

34.5cm x 30cm.

Materials

- 0.4m x 90cm calico or homespun
- Stencil film, such as Mylar
- Fine black marker pen
- Scalpel or craft knife
- Self-healing cutting board
- Acrylic paint in colours of your choice
- Fabric or textile medium
- Stencil brush
- 0.6m fine cotton cord

Method

1 PREPARATION Pre-wash, dry and press fabric. For each Bag, cut one rectangle, 32cm x 73cm.

2 CUTTING STENCILS Stencil designs are printed full size below, left. Using black marker pen, trace designs onto stencil film, then cut out carefully with a scalpel or craft knife.

3 APPLYING STENCILS Fold the fabric rectangle in half crosswise and crease. Unfold fabric and apply stencils as for **Step 3** of The Bag Bag, above, using the photograph as a guide to placement, if desired. We stencilled the mushrooms in one colour and the tiny alternating motif in a contrasting colour.

When stencilling is complete, lift stencil cleanly away and allow fabric to dry completely. Press on wrong side with a hot iron to set paint.

4 MAKING UP BAG Fold fabric in half crosswise, right sides together, and stitch sides, allowing 1cm seams. Neaten seams with zigzag or overlocking.

Press under 5mm around top edge, then press under another 1.5cm. Stitch close to inner pressed edge to form hem. Work four small thread loops 5cm below top – at sides and centre front and back. Thread cotton cord through loops and knot ends of cord. Alternatively, knot ends of cord and stitch centre of cord to one side seam, 5cm below top. Cord can then simply be wound round neck of bag to close.

Bath Sachets

Page 29

Measurements

12cm long x 7.5cm wide.

Materials

- Stencil materials, as for Mushroom Bag
- Calico or homespun
- 0.3m fine cotton cord (per sachet)
- Oatmeal or dried herbs

Method

1 PREPARATION Pre-wash, dry and press fabric. Mark fabric into 8.5cm x 26cm rectangles, with a light mark or pin at halfway point of 26cm side (fold line for front and back).

2 CUTTING STENCIL Stencil design is printed full size above. Trace and cut, as for Mushroom Bag.

3 APPLYING STENCIL Stencil motifs onto one side (front) of each sachet rectangle and set with a hot iron when dry.

4 MAKING UP BAG Cut out stencilled sachets. Press under 5mm on each narrow end, then turn under another 1.5cm and stitch. With right sides together, stitch sides, allowing 5mm seams. Turn right side out and press.

Knot ends of cord and stitch centre of cord to one side seam. Fill sachet with oatmeal or dried herbs and tie cord around top to secure.

Mouse String Minder

Page 28

Measurements

13cm wide x 16cm high.

Materials

- 16cm x 40cm cotton print
- 15cm square double-sided interfacing, such as Vliesofix
- 15cm square grey felt
- Grey embroidery cotton, optional
- Hole punch
- 5mm glass eyes or beads
- Metal eyelet, optional
- 0.25m x 13mm ribbon
- Craft glue
- Black quilting thread, for whiskers
- 1m x 5mm ribbon or thin cord
- Ball of string

Method

1 APPLIQUÉ Outline for appliqué is printed in pink on pattern sheet. Trace onto smooth side of double-sided interfacing, and cut out, leaving a margin all around. Press interfacing onto wrong side of felt square, then cut out accurately.

Fold cotton print rectangle in half crosswise, wrong sides together, and finger press to mark bottom edge of bag.

Peel backing paper from appliqué outline and press onto one side of bag, placing lower edge of mouse 1-2cm above fold line.

Open bag out flat and oversew around edge of mouse, either by hand, using blanket stitch (see **Embroidery Stitch Guide** on page 119), or by machine, using zigzag.

2 EYELET Punch a hole through both layers at indicated tail position and either insert a small metal eyelet or finish edges with blanket stitch.

3 EYES Attach glass eyes or stitch beads in position.

4 RIBBON TRIM Tie the 13mm ribbon into a bow, trim ends and glue to mouse's neck.

5 WHISKERS Cut eight x 10cm lengths of black quilting thread, knot them together in the centre and glue knot to tip of mouse's nose. To stiffen whiskers slightly, smear a little glue on your fingers and rub along length of each whisker.

6 MAKING UP BAG Fold bag in half crosswise, right sides together and, allowing 5mm seams, stitch side seams, leaving a 1cm opening in each side seam precisely 3cm from the top edge.

Press under 5mm on top edge, press under another 2cm and stitch close to edge, forming casing. Cut narrow ribbon or cord into two equal lengths and thread each piece through openings in casing from each side. Knot ends.

Place a ball of string into the bag and thread end of string out through eyelet, forming mouse's "tail".

Bread Dough Baskets

Page 30

Measurements

Baskets can be made to any size. Quantities of dough will vary according to the shape of your dishes; however, the easiest quantity to work with is the one listed below.

Materials

- 1kg plain flour
- 500g cooking salt
- 800ml hot water
- Large mixing bowl, wooden spoon and rolling pin
- Set of scales and measuring jug
- Medium-sized sharp knife
- Cling wrap
- Pastry brush
- Cooling racks
- Shapes for moulding – Pyrex/Corning Ware are best; if using tins, they will need to be lined with baking paper
- Biscuit cutter shapes, optional
- Raffia or ribbon
- Clear Gloss Estapol
- Small paintbrush

Method

1 PRE-HEAT OVEN Turn oven on to SLOW, 120°C or 250°F if baking one or two baskets, 150-160°C or 300-325°F for three or four baskets. Check your oven, as temperatures will vary.

2 MIXING DOUGH Sift flour into a large mixing bowl, add salt, then slowly pour in hot water, a little at a time, mixing as you go. When all water is poured, use your hands to combine ingredients thoroughly. Knead dough as for pastry or bread-making, about 5 minutes, or until pliable. Divide dough into two lots and set one aside, wrapped in cling wrap, for later use. If you don't divide the mixture, you will find you won't have enough room to roll it out, and it will dry before you get to mould it.

3 ROLLING DOUGH Roll dough out to approximately 2cm thick. Cut away a quarter of dough and set aside (this is for rolled braid for top edge of basket). Roll rest of dough out to a thickness of approximately 1cm.

4 CUTTING STRIPS Cut into even strips (length and width will depend on size of dish), allowing for an additional 2cm on each end of each strip to hang over edge of dish (to be cut off later).

5 PLACING STRIPS Lay first strip lengthwise along centre of dish, then start laying strips crosswise, placing first strip over centre strip, second strip under it, and so on, leaving 1.5-2cm gaps between them. Lay remaining lengthwise strips in the same fashion, starting next to existing centre strip and working towards edge on one side, then other side (**Pic 1**).

Trim excess dough from around edges, ensuring that strips go right to edge of rim of dish – if not, they will contract when baking and break away from braided edge of basket.

6 BRAIDING Cut the remaining thicker dough into strips of about 20-25cm, and roll each one into a rope shape. Take two rolls and carefully twist them around each other to form a braid (**Pic 2**). Don't try to complete circumference of basket in one go, as it will be

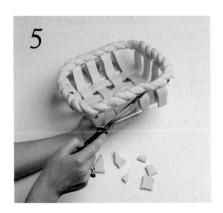

too difficult to handle – two or three braided lengths should be fine. To join braids, cut ends diagonally, dip pastry brush in water and join ends, taking care not to flatten them (**Pic 3**).

Before attaching braid to basket, use a pastry brush lightly dipped in water just to dampen rim of basket (**Pic 4**), then attach braid so that it sticks. Again, do not flatten. Tidy around edges with the help of a damp pastry brush and the point of a sharp knife (**Pic 5**).

7 BAKING If baking one or two baskets at a time, put on middle shelf of oven and bake on SLOW for 3-3½ hours, occasionally turning so that they bake evenly. If baking more than two baskets at a time, wait until you have made all baskets before putting them in the oven. Bake on SLOW for 4-5 hours, checking occasionally and turning for an even bake. Baskets must be hard, which indicates they have completely dried out – if not, they will go soft and be completely useless.

8 DECORATION With any leftover dough, you can make shapes to decorate baskets, other hand-crafted gifts, wrapped presents or the Christmas tree. Make these with biscuit cutters in whatever shapes you like. Simply cut out and place on a baking tray in the oven. These will not take as long as baskets to bake and, because they are smaller, be careful they don't burn on the bottom. A couple of hours should be sufficient to make them rock-hard. Remember, if they are to be hung or tied, you must pierce a hole through them (a skewer is ideal) before baking.

9 COOLING & SEALING Once bread dough items are baked, place on a rack to cool completely. Seal with Clear Gloss Estapol, being careful to get into cracks, applying at least three coats and allowing to dry thoroughly between coats. Sealing prevents moisture from softening the dough and allows you to wipe the baskets clean when necessary. Don't leave longer than 24 hours between baking and sealing, as the longer the bread dough is left unsealed, the greater chance that it will re-absorb moisture from the air and begin to soften.

10 FINISHING Decorate baskets with raffia or ribbon, as desired.

Etched Oil and Vinegar Bottles

Page 31

Materials

◆ Selection of clean glass jars and bottles
◆ Window cleaner or methylated spirits
◆ Self-adhesive vinyl (white or a light colour)
◆ Carbon or transfer paper
◆ Craft knife or scalpel and self-healing cutting mat
◆ Non-acid etching cream, such as Etchall
◆ Soft paintbrush

Method

1 PREPARATION Clean surface of glass with window cleaner or methylated spirits and dry with a lint-free cloth or paper towel.

2 CUTTING STENCIL Stencil outlines are printed on pattern sheet in black. Using carbon or transfer paper, trace the designs onto the white (vinyl) side of a sheet of self-adhesive vinyl and cut out carefully, using a craft knife or scalpel. Leave a large margin of uncut vinyl around the design.

3 APPLYING STENCIL Remove backing paper from stencil and apply to surface of glass, taking particular care to press down all cut edges very firmly, using the rounded end of a pencil or similar blunt instrument. Make sure you leave a good area of vinyl surrounding the stencil design to protect the glass from unwanted etching cream.

4 ETCHING Apply the etching cream thickly with a plastic spatula (never a brush) to the cut-out areas of stencil. To get an even, sharp etched image, make sure that all the design is thickly covered and that the etching cream is spread beyond the cut lines. Allow the cream to stand for 15 minutes, during which time it should not be touched.

After 15 minutes, scrape up as much etching cream as possible and return it to the container, since it can be reused. Now rinse the etched surface with running water, taking care not to allow the run-off to run on to any exposed glass.

5 FINISHING Once the glass is thoroughly rinsed, peel off the stencil and discard. Wash and dry the glass again – it is now permanently etched.

Shower Cap

Page 32

Measurements

Diameter before sewing is 58cm.

Materials

- 60cm × 90cm cotton print
- 60cm × 90cm transparent plastic
- Purchased 12mm bias binding
- 0.6m × 7mm-wide elastic
- Extra 1.5m × 12mm bias binding, for casing

Cutting

Cut one 58cm diameter circle from both cotton print and plastic.

Method

1 BINDING Place plastic circle on wrong side of fabric circle and baste together, working close to edge. (Don't pin in the middle, as the pins will leave holes in the plastic.)

Open out one edge of bias binding and, working on the fabric side of the circle, with right sides together and raw edges matching, pin, baste and sew binding to circle edge. Turn folded edge of binding around to plastic-covered circle and stitch in place, close to edge.

2 CASING Working on plastic-covered side, pin a strip of bias binding around circle, 5cm in from edge. Stitch in place close to both edges to form casing, turning in ends at centre back and leaving an opening for elastic. Thread elastic through casing, draw up to fit head, secure ends of elastic and stitch opening closed.

3 FINISHING To make bow trim, cut a 47cm length of bias binding, fold in half lengthwise and stitch edges. Tie into a bow, neaten ends and stitch to centre front of cap.

Toiletries Bag

Page 32

Measurements

Approximately 33cm x 27cm x 12cm.

Materials

- 1m × 115cm cotton print
- 1m × 115cm transparent plastic
- 50cm zip
- Bias binding

Cutting

From cotton print, cut two rectangles, each 35cm × 29cm, for bag Sides. Cut also two strips, each 53cm × 8.5cm, and one strip, 71cm × 14cm, for Gussets.

From plastic, cut a set of pieces as for fabric.

Method

1 ALIGNING PIECES Place plastic Side rectangles against the wrong side of their fabric counterparts and round off the corners.

Baste each plastic piece to the wrong side of its fabric pair, close to the outer edges. Plastic and fabric are sewn as one throughout.

2 ZIP Insert the zip between the two 53cm strips, allowing 1.5cm seam allowance, and leaving equal amounts of fabric extending at top and bottom.

3 CONTINUOUS GUSSET Fold under 1cm on one end of 71cm strip, lap this end over one end of zip and topstitch in place. Fold under 1cm on the other end of 71cm strip and lap this over the opposite end of zip, but only pin it in place as it might need adjusting.

With wrong (plastic) sides together, pin one bag Side to continuous Gusset strip, centring the zip around the top edge. Adjust length of Gusset strip if necessary and topstitch folded edge in place over raw end of zip. Baste Side in place as pinned, and repeat for remaining Side.

4 BINDING Open out one side of bias binding and fold under raw edge on end. Starting on lower edge of bag, with right sides together and raw edges even, stitch binding to bag through all layers, folding under raw end neatly when you reach the starting point again. Turn remaining folded edge of binding over raw edge and machine stitch close to folded edge. Repeat for opposite side of bag.

5 LOOP/S Make a loop for zip tab from a scrap of bias binding, and attach a second loop to lower end of zip, if desired.

Fizzy Bath Bombs

Page 32

Materials (to make 5-6 bombs)

- 1 cup bicarbonate of soda
- 1/2 cup cornflour
- 1/4 cup citric acid (see **NOTE**, below)
- Essential oil of your choice
- Food colouring
- Soap moulds (from craft stores)

NOTE. Both citric acid and bicarbonate of soda are available from baking sections of supermarkets.

Method

1 SIFTING Sift bicarbonate of soda, cornflour and citric acid into a dry bowl and mix well.

2 ESSENTIAL OIL & COLOUR Transfer half the mixture into a smaller bowl. Add 20 drops essential oil, 10 drops colouring and rub in quickly with your fingertips. Transfer mixture back to larger bowl and blend the two mixtures with your fingertips until well combined.

3 ADDING MOISTURE Transfer half the mixture back to the smaller bowl. Using a mist spray bottle, spray mixture with a little water and quickly mix with your fingertips to stop the fizzing. Add water in short sprays and mix until mixture will stay compressed when squeezed in your hand. You need very little water and it is important not to cause the mixture to fizz too much.

4 MOULDS Add a drop of essential oil to your finger and wipe around the inside of the soap moulds. Press the combined mixture firmly into the moulds. It begins to harden very quickly and, with a gentle tap, the bombs can be very carefully unmoulded onto baking paper after about 5 minutes so you can re-use the moulds for the next batch.

Repeat **Steps 3 and 4** with remaining mixture to make more bath bombs. Allow to dry completely overnight before packaging.

TIP: Flat shells and hearts are easiest to handle. The star-shaped bombs are more fragile.

Birdseed Bells

Page 42

Measurements

Can be made in any size pot, but for mass-producing, smaller is better.

Materials

- Small terracotta pots, about 7cm high
- Microwave-safe plastic wrap, or one oven bag per pot
- A length of firm wire per pot
- Pliers
- Birdseed (measure it dry in your pots to gauge amount needed)
- Two egg whites per cup of birdseed

Method

1 PREPARATION Prepare pots by lining them with microwave-safe plastic or an oven bag.

2 HANGING WIRE Cut a length of wire about 25cm long. Twist one end of wire into a flat spiral (like the coil on an electric stove), slightly smaller than diameter of top of the pot. Twist the coil so that it lies at right angles to the remaining wire stem.

3 MIXTURE Beat egg whites until white and fluffy (but not stiff). Mix beaten egg whites and birdseed in a bowl until all seed is coated, then spoon this mixture into prepared pots, patting it down firmly.

Push uncoiled end of wire through centre of pot, down through mixture and out of pot drainage hole until coiled end rests flat on top of mixture. Push coil slightly into mixture.

4 BAKING Place on an oven shelf set high enough to allow wire to hang free. Cook for about 1-1½ hours in a very cool oven. The important thing is not to burn the mixture – slow cooking is what is needed to set it firmly.

5 FINISHING Cooked bells will slip easily from pots. Peel away plastic wrap from sides of bells while they're still warm, but don't handle wire until it has cooled. Using a pair of pliers, twist end of wire into a hook for hanging.

TIP: Sometimes, if you are using large seeds in your mixture, the widest part of the bell (exposed during cooking) seems to dry out and become slightly crumbly. This only happens for a centimetre or two, but to prevent it happening you can do the following: Spoon mixture into pot as usual, but mix another beaten egg white with seeds of last few centimetres, then cook as instructed. This extra "adhesive" keeps top layer very firm.

Cross Stitched Garden Gloves

Page 43

Measurements

Motif measures 3.5cm wide x 8cm high.

Materials

- Cotton gardening gloves (see NOTE, below)
- Small amount waste canvas
- One skein DMC Stranded Embroidery Cotton in each of the following colours: v. light mahogany 402, v. dark blue-green 500, fern green 522, v. dark drab brown 610, v. light terracotta 758, light copper 922, dark red-copper 918 and dark hunter green 3345
- Embroidery needle
- 0.2m x 90cm knit ribbing (optional)

NOTE. Choose gloves that do not have seams in the cross stitch area. Ours cost less than $2 at a nursery, but the cuffs were bright red, so we bought a small amount of knit ribbing and changed them to green.

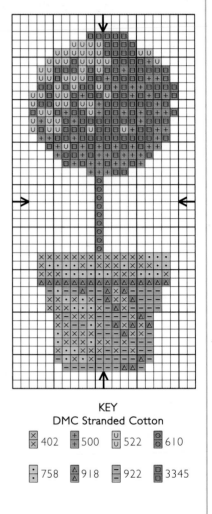

Cross Stitch Graph for Gardening Glove

KEY
DMC Stranded Cotton

× 402	+ 500	U 522	o 610
· 758	▲ 918	– 922	▢ 3345

Method

1 WASTE CANVAS Baste a scrap of waste canvas to the back of each glove, taking care that it is centred and big enough to contain motif (count the squares – the design is 40 stitches high x 18 stitches wide).

2 CROSS STITCH Using three strands of thread and following graph and key above, work cross stitch (see **Embroidery Stitch Guide** on page 119) onto waste canvas, stitching through all layers and taking care not to catch waste canvas in the stitches.

When embroidery is complete, remove basting, then pull out waste canvas thread by thread (tweezers can help), leaving the cross stitched motif on the glove.

3 CUFFS (OPTIONAL) If desired, carefully unpick cuffs from gloves and use as a pattern to cut two new ones. Stitch new cuffs to gloves, stretching them to fit as you sew.

Gardener's Hand Balm

Page 43

Materials

- 25g anhydrous lanolin (from a chemist)
- 10g pure beeswax
- 1/4 teaspoon borax
- 75ml almond oil
- 50ml rose water
- One 400 IU vitamin E capsule
- 10 drops lavender essential oil
- 5 drops eucalyptus oil
- 5 drops rosemary essential oil

Method

1 MIXING Melt lanolin and beeswax in a double pan over low heat. Remove from heat and stir in borax until it is dissolved.

2 BEATING Slowly add almond oil while beating with a hand-held electric whisk. Add rosewater while continuing to whisk – the mixture will gradually thicken and combine to a smooth, creamy consistency.

3 FINISHING Break open the vitamin E capsule and add to the cream mixture, along with the three essential oils. Mix thoroughly and transfer to a small, clean sterilised jar. Seal jar immediately.

Crocheted Finger Puppets

Page 46

Materials

- Scraps of 5-ply yarn (if you only have 8-ply, unravel one strand and use remaining yarn)
- 3.00mm crochet hook
- Tapestry needle

Tension

See **Knitting and Crochet Notes** on page 119. 5dc to 2cm.

Method

BASIC PUPPET

Using first colour (C1), make 17ch, *turn*, 1dc in 2nd ch from hook, 1dc in each ch to end…16dc.

Work a further 5 rows in C1 (6 rows in all for Body).

Crochet Body in one colour and decorate as desired with embroidered patches or buttons; or crochet in stripes, using one colour per row.

Change to face colour (C2) and work 5 rows, then change to hair colour (C3) and work 3 rows. Fasten off.

(Note that for all animals, you do not change to C3, but continue with C2).

At centre front, embroider eyes with French knots (see **Embroidery Stitch Guide** on page 119) and mouth with back stitch (people only), leaving opening at back of head. For Wolf eyes, stitch white background first, to accentuate size.

Fold in half, right sides together, and stitch centre back seam. Run a gathering thread around top edge, pull up tightly and fasten off securely.

HAIR (for People)

Cut lengths of yarn twice the desired finished length of hair. Fold lengths in half and tie a knot in the centre to secure. Stitch hair to head, then style as desired.

EARS (for Pig, Bears and Wolf)

Make 4ch, *turn*, 1dc into 2nd ch from hook, 1dc into each ch to end…3dc.

2nd row. 1dc into 2nd ch from hook, fasten off.

SNOUT (for Bears, Pigs)

Make 3ch and join into a circle.

1st row. 4dc into circle.

2nd row. 2dc into each dc…8dc. Fasten off.

Stitch Snout to face and embroider as photographed.

SNOUT (for Wolf)

Work as for Bear Snout, above, but add an extra 3 rows before fastening off (8dc per row). Attach to face and embroider teeth and tongue as photographed.

WITCH

Work as for Basic Puppet until 5 rows of C2 are complete.

Change to hat colour and work 3 rows. Decrease by working 1dc into every 2nd dc until 1dc remains. Fasten off.

BRIM

Using hat colour, make 3ch, *turn*, 1dc into 2nd ch from hook, 1dc into rem ch…2dc.

2nd row. 1ch, 1dc into each dc to end…2dc. Rep 2nd row until strip will fit around head. Fasten off. Stitch to head, joining ends at centre back.

WITCH'S NOSE

Using C2, make 5ch, *turn*, 1dc into 2nd ch from hook, 1dc into each ch to end…4dc. Fasten off. Fold long edges together and stitch, forming long nose. Stitch to face.

Crocheted Lion Puppet

Page 46

Measurements

Approximately 30cm tall.

Materials

8-ply acrylic (we used Panda Disco), 20g balls:
- **1st Contrast Colour** (C1, orange): 3 balls
- **2nd Contrast Colour** (C2, yellow): 2 balls
- **3rd Contrast Colour** (C3, cream): small amount
- **4th Contrast Colour** (C4, tan): small amount
- 3.00mm crochet hook
- 30cm square fabric for lining
- 10cm-diameter polystyrene ball
- Small amount polyester fibrefill
- Tapestry needle
- One pair 1cm-diameter joggle eyes
- Craft glue

Pattern piece

Pattern piece is printed on the pattern sheet in a pink tone. Trace Puppet Body Front/Back.

Cutting

NOTE. 5mm seam allowance is **included** on all edges, except centre back, where allowance should be added when cutting.

From lining fabric, cut one Body Front on the fold, and two Body Backs.

Tension

See **Knitting and Crochet Notes** on page 119. 24sts and 24 rows to 10cm over double crochet.

HEAD

Using 3.00mm hook and C2 yarn, make 4ch and join with sl st to form a ring.

1st rnd. Work 8dc into ring, join with a sl st. (Join each rnd with a sl st throughout).

2nd rnd. 2dc into each dc of previous rnd…16dc.

3rd rnd. *2dc in next dc, 1dc in next dc, rep from * to end…24dc.

4th and each alt rnd. 1dc in each dc to end.

5th rnd. *2dc in next dc, 1dc in each of next 2dc, rep from * to end…32dc.

7th rnd. *2dc in next dc, 1dc in each of next 3dc, rep from * to end…40dc.

Cont in this manner, working 1 extra dc between incs until end of 13th rnd…64dc.

Work 15 rnds without shaping.

With a small, sharp kitchen knife, cut a hole in polystyrene ball, about 3cm in diameter and 4cm deep. Place polystyrene ball inside Head and continue in dc, dec instead of inc on each alt row thus:

29th rnd. *Work 2dc tog (dec), 1dc in each of next 6dc, rep from * to end…56dc.

Cont in this manner to end of 35th rnd (32 sts rem). Fasten off. Turn ball, if necessary, so that hole faces neck edge.

BODY

Using 3.00mm hook and C1, make 4ch and join with a sl st to form a ring.

1st rnd. Work 8dc into ring, join with a sl st . (Join each subsequent round with a sl st.)

2nd rnd. 2dc in each dc of previous rnd…16dc.

3rd rnd. *2dc in next dc, 1dc in next dc. rep from * to end…24dc.

4th rnd. 1dc in each dc to end.

Change to rows instead of rounds, to form back opening.

5th row. *2dc in next dc, 1dc in each of next 2dc, rep from * to end, *turn*…32dc.

6th and alternate rows. Work in dc without shaping.

Cont working in rows, but shaping as for Head until end of 13th row…64dc.

Divide for armholes. 25th row. 1dc in each of first 19dc, *turn*. Work a further 9 rows on these sts only. Fasten off.

Rejoin yarn to 25th row and work 10 rows over next 26 sts, fasten off, then work 10 rows on rem 19 sts.

Change to rnds, working next rnd as for 29th rnd of Head and dec every alternate rnd until 39th rnd has been completed. Fasten off.

ARM/LEG (make 4)

Using 3.00mm hook and C3, make 4ch, join with sl st to form ring.

1st rnd. Work 8dc into ring.

2nd rnd. 2dc in each dc to end…16dc.

3rd rnd. 1dc in each dc to end.

4th rnd. *2dc in next dc, 1dc in next dc, rep from * to end…24dc.

5th rnd. As 3rd rnd.

Change to C2. Work 10 rnds dc without shaping. Fasten off.

EARS (make 4)

Using 3.00mm hook and C2, make 11ch, turn.

1st row. Miss 1ch, 1dc in each ch to end…10dc. Work 3 rows dc without shaping.

5th row. Miss first dc, 1dc in each dc to last dc, miss last dc…8dc.

Rep last row until 2 sts rem. Fasten off.

SNOUT

Using 3.00mm hook and C4, make 4ch, join with a sl st to form ring.

1st rnd. Work 8dc into ring.

2nd and 3rd rnds. 1dc in each dc to end.

4th rnd. 2dc in each dc to end…16dc.

5th rnd. 1dc in each dc to end.

Break off tan yarn and join in C3.

6th to 10th rnds. Work as 3rd to 7th rnds of Head.

Work a further 2 rnds in dc without shaping. Fasten off.

MANE

Using 3.00mm hook, attach C1 with a sl st to centre front neck position of Head.

1st rnd. *4ch, miss 3dc, sl st into next dc, rep from * around face, making approximately 19 4ch-loops, join with a sl st.

2nd rnd. *10ch, 1dc in next dc, rep from *, making 10ch-loops in every dc to end. Fasten off.

Rep 1st rnd, approximately 2.5cm behind first rnd of Mane.

4th rnd. *15ch, 1dc in next dc, rep from *, making 15ch-loops in every dc to end. Fasten off.

To make up

Place 2 Ear sections tog and, using C3, work 1 row dc around shaped edges to join them. Gather around outer edges to form cup shape and attach commencing ch to Head, placing Ears between 2 rnds of Mane.

With right sides together, join Head and Body sections together. Place small amount fibrefill in each Leg, close opening and stitch Legs to Body. Using C4, embroider claws as photographed.

With right sides together, stitch Arms to armholes. Fill Snout with fibrefill and stitch to Head. Glue on eyes and embroider mouth as photographed, using C4.

With right sides together, matching Arms, stitch lining Body Front to lining Body Back around outer edges, leaving neck edge open and centre back seam open between dots.

Insert a small amount of fibrefill into crocheted body cavity to give it a little shape, then place lining inside crocheted body, wrong sides facing. Turn under seam allowance on raw edges of lining and slipstitch folded edges in place around back opening and around inside edge of neck opening.

Knitted Cat

Page 47

Measurements

Approximately 26cm long to base of tail.

Materials

8-ply wool (we used Patons Totem), 50g balls:

- ◆ **1st Contrast Colour** (C1, aqua): 3 balls
- ◆ **2nd Contrast Colour** (C2, olive): 3 balls
- ◆ **3rd Contrast Colour** (C3, purple): 1 ball
- ◆ **4th Contrast Colour** (C4, black): small amount
- ◆ **5th Contrast Colour** (C5, pink): small amount
- ◆ **6th Contrast Colour** (C6, yellow): small amount
- ◆ One pair each 7.50mm (No 1) and 4.00mm (No 8) knitting needles
- ◆ Three safety pins
- ◆ Polyester fibrefill
- ◆ Knitter's needle or tapestry needle for seams and embroidery

Tension

See **Knitting and Crochet Notes** on page 119. 12 sts and 17.5 rows to 10cm over st st, using 7.50mm needles and yarn tripled.

NOTE. This toy has been designed using yarn tripled throughout.

FRONT (beg with Legs)

Using 7.50mm needles and C1, cast on 5 sts.

NOTE. Do not weave colours in Fair Isle patt, but carry colour not in use loosely across on wrong side of work. Always carry colours to ends of rows and always carry C1 above C2.

1st row. (K1 C1, K1 C2) twice, K1 C1.
2nd row. (P1 C1, P1 C2) twice, P1 C1.
Rep these 2 rows until work measures 11cm from beg, ending with a 2nd row.

Break off yarn, leave sts on a safety pin. Work other 3 Legs in same manner, noting to leave 4th Leg sts on needle.

Cont for Body as folls. 1st row. Work across 4th Leg sts as folls – K3 C2, K2 C1, cast on one st in C1 and 2 sts in C2, knit across 5 sts from safety pin as folls – K1 C2, K3 C1, K1 C2, cast on 2 sts in C2, 3 sts in C1, 3 sts in C2 and 2 sts in C1, knit across 5 Leg sts from safety pin as folls – K1 C1, K3 C2, K1 C1, cast on 2 sts in C1 and one st in C2, knit across 5 Leg sts from rem safety pin as folls – K2 C2, K3 C1…36 sts.
2nd row. (P3 C1, P3 C2) 6 times.
3rd row. (K3 C2, K3 C1) 6 times.
4th row. (P3 C2, P3 C1) 6 times.
5th row. (K3 C1, K3 C2) 6 times.
6th row. As 4th row.**
7th row. As 3rd row.
Last 6 rows form patt.
Work a further 5 rows in patt, dec one st at beg of next and foll alt rows 3 times in all…33 sts.
13th row. K15 C2, patt to last 2 sts, K2tog.
14th row. Patt to last 15 sts, P15 C2.
Rep 13th and 14th rows once, then 13th row once…30 sts.
Cast off 15 sts in patt, then purl to end in C2. Break off C1.
Cont on last 15 sts in C2 for Head.
Work 8 rows st st.
Shape top. Dec one st at each end of every row 4 times…7 sts.
Cast off.

BACK

Work as for Front to **.
Keeping chequerboard patt correct for rem of Back, dec one st at beg of next and foll alt rows 6 times in all…30 sts.
Work one row.
Next row. Cast off 15 sts for Back, patt to end…15 sts.
Cont on last 15 sts for Head.
Work 7 rows patt.
Shape top. Dec one st at each end of every row 4 times…7 sts.
Cast off.

TAIL

Using 7.50mm needles and C1, cast on 6 sts.
Work 36 rows st st in stripes of 4 rows C1 and 2 rows C2.
Work 4 rows C1.
Cast off.

RIGHT EAR (beg at base)

Using 7.50mm needles and C1, cast on 6 sts.
1st row. K4, K2tog.
2nd row. P2tog, P3.
3rd row. K2, K2tog.
4th row. P2tog, P1.
5th row. K2tog. Fasten off.

LEFT EAR (beg at base)

Using 7.50mm needles and C1, cast on 6 sts.
1st row. K2tog, K4.
2nd row. P3, P2tog.
3rd row. K2tog, K2.
4th row. P1, P2tog.
5th row. K2tog. Fasten off.

COLLAR

Using 4.00mm needles and one strand of C3, cast on 70 sts.
Work 4 rows garter st (1st row is wrong side). Cast off.

To make up

Using back stitch, join Front and Back tog, leaving an opening for filling. Turn right side out, fill firmly and close opening. Using one strand of C4 and stem stitch (see **Embroidery Stitch Guide** on page 119), embroider facial features as shown in photograph. Using one strand of C5 and satin stitch, embroider cheeks. Using satin stitch and C6, attach Collar to neck of Cat by working a fake buckle as shown in photograph. Catch Collar to Cat at sides and back of neck. Stitch long edges of Tail tog, drawing up sts slightly so that Tail curls. Stitch Ears and Tail in position.

Knitted Bird

Page 47

Measurements

Approximately 36cm (from tip of beak to tail).

Materials

8-ply wool (we used Patons Totem), 50g balls:
- ◆ **1st Contrast Colour** (C1, yellow): 1 ball
- ◆ **2nd Contrast Colour** (C2, red): 1 ball
- ◆ **3rd Contrast Colour** (C3, blue): 1 ball
- ◆ **4th Contrast Colour** (C4, black): small amount
- ◆ One pair 7.50mm (No 1) knitting needles
- ◆ Yarn bobs
- ◆ One stitch-holder
- ◆ One 6.50mm (No 4) crochet hook
- ◆ Polyester fibrefill
- ◆ Knitter's needle or tapestry needle for seams and embroidery

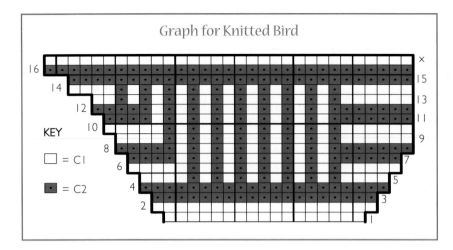

Graph for Knitted Bird

KEY

☐ = C1

▨ = C2

Tension

See **Knitting and Crochet Notes** on page 119. 12 sts and 17.5 rows to 10cm over st st, using 7.50mm needles and yarn tripled.

NOTE. This toy has been designed using yarn tripled throughout.

BODY (beg at lower edge)

Using 7.50mm needles and C1, cast on 17 sts.
Beg Graph. NOTE. This toy has been worked using both Fair Isle and Colour Change methods. When working in Fair Isle patt, do not weave colours, but carry colour not in use loosely across on wrong side of work. Always carry colours to ends of rows and always carry C1 above C2. When using Colour Change method and changing colours in middle of row, twist colour to be used (on wrong side) underneath and to right of colour just used. Use a separate ball of yarn for each section of colour by winding small amounts of yarn onto yarn bobs.
1st row. Knit.
2nd row. Inc one st in first st, purl to last st, inc one st in last st…19 sts.
Work rows 3 to 16 incl from Graph (see above), noting incs and to work odd-numbered rows (knit rows) from right to left, and even-numbered rows (purl rows) from left to right…31 sts.
17th row. Using C1, K11 and leave these 11 sts on a stitch-holder for Head, knit across rem 20 sts for Back.
Next row. Using C1, P20, *turn*, cast on 11 sts…31 sts.
Work other side of Bird by reading Graph from 16th row to 1st row as folls:
16th row. Using C2, knit.
15th row. Using C2, cast off 2 sts , purl to end…29 sts.
14th row. Using C1, patt to end.
13th row. Using C1, cast off 2 sts, patt across rem sts foll Graph…27 sts.
Cont working from Graph as placed in last 4 rows until 1st row has been completed…17 sts.

HEAD

Slip 11 sts from stitch-holder to 7.50mm needle. Using C1, work in st st until Head measures 4cm, ending with a purl row.
Tie a marker at Front edge of Head to indicate top of Beak.
Dec one st at each end of alt rows twice…7 sts.
Cast off.
With right side facing, using 7.50mm needles and C1, knit up 11 sts evenly along cast-on edge for other side of Head.
Work to correspond with other side of Head.
Using back stitch, join Head halves tog from markers to Back.

BEAK

With right side of Bird facing, using 7.50mm needles and C2, beg at point X marked on Graph and knit up 11 sts to point X marked on Graph on Back, knitting up centre st from Head seam.
Work 3 rows st st, beg with a purl row.
4th row. K3, K2tog, K1, K2tog, K3…9 sts.
Work 3 rows st st, beg with a purl row.
8th row. K2, K2tog, K1, K2tog, K2…7 sts.
Work 3 rows st st, beg with a purl row.
12th row. (K1, K2tog) twice, K1…5 sts.
Work 3 rows st st, beg with a purl row.
16th row. K2tog, K1, K2tog…3 sts.
17th row. P3tog. Fasten off.

To make up

Cut 20cm lengths of C1 for Crest. Using hook, draw 2 strands halfway through a st at top of Head and knot both halves of strands tog twice. Rep this 16 times to form Crest as shown in photograph.
Using chain stitch (see **Embroidery Stitch Guide** on page 119) and a single strand of C3, embroider eyes as photographed. Using a single strand of C4, work a French knot to centre of each eye. Using a single strand of C3, work satin stitch to centre of each eye as photographed.
Using a single strand of C3, work stem stitch block patt to Body as shown. Join Beak seam, leaving an opening, fill lightly, close opening. Using back stitch, join rem of Bird, leaving an opening for filling. Fill, then close opening.

Knitted Rabbit

Page 47

Measurements

Approximately 43cm high.

Materials

8-ply wool (we used Patons Totem), 50g balls:
◆ 1st Contrast Colour (C1, white): 2 balls
◆ 2nd Contrast Colour (C2, red): 1 ball
◆ 3rd Contrast Colour (C3, yellow): 1 ball
◆ 4th Contrast Colour (C4, pink): 1 ball
◆ 5th Contrast Colour (C5, green): 1 ball
◆ 6th Contrast Colour (C6, burnt orange): 1 ball
◆ 7th Contrast Colour (C7, black): small amount for embroidery
◆ One pair each 7.50mm (No 1) and 4.00mm (No 8) knitting needles
◆ One safety pin
◆ Polyester fibrefill
◆ Knitter's needle or tapestry needle for seams and embroidery

Tension

See **Knitting and Crochet Notes** on page 119. 12 sts and 17.5 rows to 10cm over st st, using 7.50mm needles and yarn tripled.

NOTE. This toy has been designed using yarn tripled throughout.

FRONT

RIGHT LEG (beg at foot)
Using 7.50mm needles and C1, cast on 11 sts. Work 5 rows st st.
6th row. Cast off 5 sts, purl to end…6 sts. Break off C1.

NOTE. Do not weave colours in Fair Isle patt, but carry colour not in use loosely across on wrong side of work. Always carry colours to end of rows and always carry C2 above C3, and C4 above C5.

7th row. K3 C3, K3 C2.
8th row. P3 C2, P3 C3.
9th row. As 7th row.
10th row. P3 C3, P3 C2.
11th row. K3 C2, K3 C3.
12th row. As 10th row.
Rows 7 to 12 incl form Leg patt.
Work a further 6 rows patt.
Leave sts on a safety pin.

LEFT LEG

Using 7.50mm needles and C1, cast on 11 sts.
Work 5 rows st st, beg with a purl row.
6th row. Cast off 5 sts, K2 C2, K3 C3...6 sts.
Break off C1.
7th row. P3 C3, P3 C2.
8th row. K3 C2, K3 C3.
Work a further 9 rows Leg Patt as for Right Leg as *placed* in last 3 rows.
Beg Body. 1st row. Work across Left Leg sts as folls – K3 C2, K3 C3, using C2 cast on 3 sts, work across Right Leg sts as folls – K3 C3, K3 C2...15 sts.
Keeping patt correct, work 5 rows.
Break off C2 and C3.
Beg Shirt. 1st row. K1 C4, (K1 C5, K1 C4) 7 times.
2nd row. P1 C4, (P1 C5, P1 C4) 7 times.
Last 2 rows form patt for Shirt.
Rep 1st and 2nd rows once.
Tie a coloured thread at each end of last row to mark the armholes.
Cont in patt until Body measures 11cm from top of Legs, ending with a 2nd row.
Shape shoulders. Keeping patt correct, cast off 2 sts at beg of next 2 rows...11 sts.
Break off C4 and C5.
Beg Head. Using C1, work in st st until Head measures 7.5cm, ending with a purl row.
Cast off.

BACK

Work to correspond with Front, using **C2** in place of C3, and **C3** in place of C2, thus reversing colours.
Using back stitch, join Front and Back tog around Head and shoulders only.

LEFT ARM

With right side facing and using 7.50mm needles, knit up 10 sts evenly along Front and Back left armhole, beg at coloured thread at Front as folls: (K1 C5, K1 C4) 5 times.
Cont in Shirt patt until Arm measures 5cm from pick-up, ending with a 2nd row.
Cast off.

RIGHT ARM

Work to correspond with Left Arm.
Cast off.

EARS (beg at base, make 2)

Using 7.50mm needles and C1, cast on 8 sts.
1st row. (K1, yft, sl 1 purlways, ybk) 4 times.
Rep last row until work measures 9cm from beg.
Break off yarn, leaving a 25cm-long thread end. Using knitter's needle, run end through 1st, 3rd, 5th and 7th sts on needle, slip all sts off needle and place rem 4 sts back on needle. Pull yarn firmly, then starting with 8th st, run knitter's needle through 4 sts on needle. Slip these 4 sts off needle, pull yarn firmly and fasten off. Sew Ears to Head.

CARROT (make 3)

Using 4.00mm needles and single strand of C6, cast on 5 sts.
Work 2 rows st st.
Inc one st at each end of next and foll alt rows until there are 13 sts, then in foll 4th rows until there are 17 sts.
Work 7 rows. Cast off.

To make up

Stitch rem of Rabbit tog, leaving an opening. Fill firmly and close opening. Using a single strand of C7, embroider mouth, nose and eyes in stem stitch and satin stitch (see **Embroidery Stitch Guide** on page 119). Using a single strand of C2 and satin stitch, embroider cheeks. Join side seam of Carrots, leaving an opening for filling. Fill firmly and close opening. Catch short lengths of C5 to top of Carrots, if desired. Using C5, bind Carrot tops tog. Stitch Carrots to Arm as shown in photograph.

Lizard Paperweight

Page 48

Measurements

26cm long.

Materials

◆ Small amount printed satin
◆ Small amount contrast plain satin
◆ Two small black glass beads
◆ Fine sand or millet
◆ Tiny funnel (optional)

Pattern pieces

All pattern pieces are printed on pattern sheet in a grey tone. Trace Lizard Upper Body and Underbody.

Cutting

NOTE. There is no seam allowance added to these patterns. To give yourself an accurate sewing line, cut the pattern pieces from cardboard or firm paper, place them on fabric then trace around outline with something that will show clearly on the fabric. Cut out roughly, leaving adequate allowance, but do not attempt to cut accurately until after sewing is completed, when you can use small sharp scissors to cut around seams, snip into stitching on tight curves and cut away excess fabric.

From satin print, cut two Lizard Upper Bodies, remembering to add seam allowance.
From contrast satin, cut one Lizard Underbody, remembering to add seam allowance.

Method

1 UPPER BODY With right sides together, and using a small, straight machine stitch, sew upper Body sections together, from tip of nose, around upper edge to tip of tail. This forms complete Upper Body.

2 UNDERBODY With right sides together, stitch Upper Body to Underbody, leaving a small opening on one side of belly, for turning. When sewing is complete, use small sharp scissors to trim seam allowance to 3mm, clip into stitching on tight curves and notch remaining curves, taking care all the time not to cut stitching line. Turn right side out.

3 FILLING If you don't have a miniature funnel, such as those used to fill perfume atomisers, you can easily make a tight paper cone and snip off one end, leaving a small hole. Put end of funnel into lizard to test its size, then, before filling, slipstitch opening closed a little, so that it just accommodates end of funnel. Pour sand or millet gently into lizard, making sure to work it into the tail and toes as you go. Don't fill too tightly – the completed lizard should be slightly squashy, not rigid. Carefully withdraw funnel and slipstitch remainder of opening closed, using tiny stitches so filling can't escape.

4 FINISHING Stitch a small black bead eye securely to each side of lizard's head.

Calico School Dolls

Page 49

Measurements

Approximately 50cm high.

Materials

DOLL (Materials for one doll)
- 0.9m x 115cm unbleached calico or cream homespun
- Polyester fibrefill
- Fine brown fabric pen
- Red coloured pencil or blusher
- Sewing thread
- One ball acrylic yarn for hair
- Craft glue

CLOTHES (Girl)
- 0.5m x 90cm small check or uniform fabric (we cut up an old uniform)
- 0.25m x 115cm lightweight plain contrast fabric, for Collar and Knickers
- 0.7m x 90cm cotton drill, for Hat
- 15cm zip

- Purchased bias binding, or cut a bias strip from uniform fabric
- Pair of Size 00 baby socks or doll socks
- 30cm square black felt, for Shoes
- 0.6m x 7mm-wide elastic
- Black wool for shoelaces
- Hair ribbons

CLOTHES (Boy)
- 0.25m x 115cm stretch knit, for polo shirt (we cut up an old school polo shirt)
- 0.1m contrast knit ribbing or double knit collar from old polo shirt
- 25cm x 60cm grey cotton drill, for Shorts
- 0.7m x 90cm cotton drill, for Hat
- 0.3cm x 1cm-wide elastic
- Two small buttons
- Two metal snap fasteners, Size 000
- Pair of Size 00 baby socks or doll socks
- 30cm square black felt, for Shoes
- Black wool for shoelaces
- Fabric pen (to match school colours)

Pattern pieces

All pattern pieces are printed on the pattern sheet in black. Trace Front Head 1, Back Head 2, Chin 3, Ear 4, Front Body 5, Back Body 6, Bottom 7, Arm 8, Leg 9, Dress/Polo Shirt Front 10, Dress Back 11, Dress/Polo Shirt Sleeve 12, Collar 13, Tie 14, Placket 15, Shorts/Knickers 16, Pocket 17, Hat Crown 18, Hat Brim 19, Hat Side 20, Shoe Upper 21 and Shoe Sole 22.

Cutting

NOTE. All pattern pieces **include** 5mm seam allowance unless otherwise indicated.

From calico, cut one Front Head, two Back Heads, one Chin, four Ears, one Front Body, two Back Bodies, one Bottom, four Arms and four Legs.

From checked fabric, cut one Dress Front, two Dress Backs and two Sleeves.

From contrast fabric, cut two Knickers/Shorts, four Collars and two Ties.

From stretch cotton knit, cut two Polo Shirt Fronts (front and back are identical), and one Placket.

From grey cotton drill cut two Knickers/Shorts and one Pocket.

From cotton drill, cut two Hat Crowns, two Hat Brims and one Hat Side (for each hat).

From black felt, cut four Shoe Uppers and two Shoe Soles (for each pair of shoes).

Method

NOTE. All pieces are joined with right sides together and 5mm seams, unless otherwise indicated.

DOLL

1 FACE Using the Front Head pattern piece as a guide, draw eyes, nose and mouth onto Front Head with brown fabric pen. If you are not confident, place pattern piece and Front Head over a strong light, such as on a glass coffee table with lamp beneath, or against a well-lit window and trace the face details onto the fabric. Heat set, if necessary, and set aside.

2 EARS Stitch Ears together in pairs, leaving straight edge open. Trim seam, clip curves, turn Ears right side out and press. With right sides together and raw edges matching, baste Ears in position on Front Head.

3 HEAD Stitch Back Heads together at centre back seam. With right sides together, stitch dart in Front Head. Matching centre notches and large dots, stitch Front Head to Chin. Matching symbols, stitch Front Head to Back Head, sandwiching raw edges of Ears at the same time and leaving neck edge open. Turn completed head right side out and set aside.

4 ARMS Stitch Arms together in pairs. Clip curves, turn right side out and stuff firmly with fibrefill. Baste across raw edges to hold, matching seam lines at the centre of each Arm. Set aside.

5 LEGS With right sides together, stitch dart in foot of each Leg. Stitch Legs together in pairs, matching foot darts and leaving top straight edge open. Clip curves, turn Legs right side out and stuff firmly with fibrefill. Baste across raw edges to hold, matching seam lines at the centre of each Leg. Set aside.

6 BODY Stitch Back Bodies together at centre back seam. Stitch Back Body to Front Body at shoulder seams. With right sides together, raw edges matching, and taking care

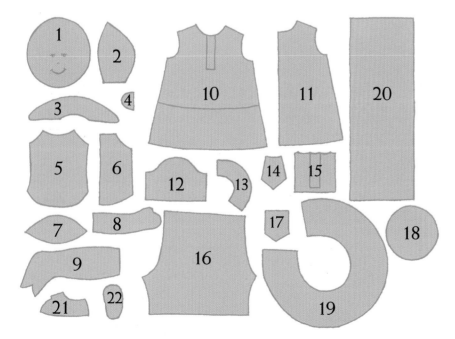

that thumbs face toward the front, baste an Arm in indicated position on each side of Front Body. Stitch side seams, sandwiching raw edges of Arms at the same time.

Matching raw edges, centre front dots and centre back seams, baste then stitch head to body around neck edge. With right sides together and matching raw edges, baste Legs in indicated position on lower Front Body. Matching notches at centre front and matching large dot to centre back seam, baste then stitch Bottom to lower edge of body, sandwiching raw edges of Legs at the same time and leaving open between small dots in back seam. Turn right side out.

7 STUFFING Fill doll with fibrefill through opening in lower edge, stuffing the head firmly first, making sure that neck area is very firmly stuffed. Stuff body firmly, turn in raw edges of opening and slipstitch opening closed.

8 HAIR Cut a strip of calico or homespun on the bias, about 4cm wide x 15cm long. Cut a number of 40cm lengths of acrylic yarn – the exact number will depend on how thick your yarn is and how thick you want the hair to be, but you need enough to fit side by side along the length of bias strip, leaving 1.5cm fabric extending at each end. Using a little craft glue, position yarn lengths across strip, so that yarn ends extend evenly on each side of strip. Using a thread that matches hair, machine stitch along centre of strip to secure yarn, then stitch again a couple more times, close to the first line of stitching. Fold under extending calico ends so they are concealed and glue them in place.

Positioning one end of strip in centre of seam line between Front and Back Head pieces, glue strip in place down back of head towards nape of neck. Allow to dry completely. Pull some of the yarn from each side around to front and trim into a fringe, dabbing a little glue on forehead to keep in place, if necessary. Trim and style rest of hair as you wish, using a sparing amount of glue to fix it in place underneath if needed.

9 FINISHING Use blusher or smudged red pencil to add a little colour to the cheeks and use the tip of the fabric pen to dot tiny freckles across the bridge of the nose and cheeks – don't overdo it.

CLOTHES

NOTE. All pieces are joined with right sides together and 5mm seams, unless otherwise indicated.

1 KNICKERS Press under 5mm on leg edge of each Knicker piece, then press under the remaining casing allowance along fold line and stitch close to inner edge, forming casing. Cut two pieces of 7mm elastic to fit around each leg, stretching slightly. Thread elastic through casing. Secure one end with a couple of rows

of stitching at start of casing. Pull remaining end through casing and secure as before.

Stitch inside leg seams, sandwiching raw ends of elastic in the seam. Place one leg inside the other, right sides together, and stitch crotch seam from centre front to centre back, matching inside leg seams. Press under 1cm on upper raw edge, then turn under another 1cm and stitch to form casing, leaving an opening at centre back to thread elastic.

Cut a piece of 7mm elastic to fit doll's waist, thread through casing, secure ends and stitch opening closed.

2 DRESS Allowing a 1.5cm seam, stitch Dress Backs together at centre back seam, leaving open above small dot for zip. Insert zip in centre back opening. Stitch Front to Back at shoulder seams.

Press 5mm on lower Sleeve edge to *right* side, then press another 1.5cm to *right* side, forming cuff on outside of Sleeve. Topstitch close to both edges of cuffs. Repeat for second Sleeve. (Note that this way of forming a cuff will only work if fabric is the same on both sides. If you have chosen fabric with an obvious right and wrong side, simply press under a hem and secure with two rows of topstitching.)

Run a line of ease stitching around the crown of each Sleeve, between dots. With centre of Sleeve matching shoulder seam and adjusting ease stitching to fit if necessary, stitch Sleeves to armholes.

Stitch sleeve and side seam in one continuous operation, matching sleeve seams.

Stitch Ties together, leaving neck edge open. Clip corners, turn right side out and press. With raw edges even and matching small dot to centre front of dress, baste Tie to neck edge of dress.

Stitch Collars together in pairs, leaving neck edge open. Clip curves and corners, turn Collars right side out and press. Baste Collars to neck edge of dress with raw edges even, and front edges almost meeting at centre front of Tie. Cut a piece of bias binding (or a narrow bias strip of dress fabric) to fit neck edge, plus extra for turning). Open out one edge of binding and, with right sides together and raw edges even, stitch binding to neck edge through all layers, sandwiching Collars and Tie at the same time. Turn binding to inside and slipstitch remaining edge in place, folding in raw ends at centre back to neaten.

Turn up hem on lower edge of dress and slipstitch in place.

3 SHORTS Press under 1cm on upper edge of Pocket and topstitch close to folded edge, then again, 5mm from first stitching. Press under 5mm on remaining raw edges of Pocket and topstitch Pocket in indicated position on back of one Shorts Front/Back section.

Finish lower edges of Shorts Front/Back sections with a narrow zigzag. Press under hem

allowance along given fold line, then topstitch hem in place close to zigzagged edge and again 2mm from first stitching. Stitch inside leg seams. Stitch crotch seam from centre front to centre back, matching inside leg seams.

Press under 5mm on upper raw edge, then turn under another 1.5cm and stitch to form casing, leaving an opening at centre back to thread elastic. Cut a piece of 1cm elastic to fit doll's waist, thread through casing, secure ends and stitch opening closed.

Press pleats in centre front of each trouser leg.

4 POLO SHIRT Transfer stitching and slash lines to wrong side of Placket, using tailor's chalk or light pencil. With *right* side of Placket facing *wrong* side of one Shirt Front (remaining section will be called the Back from now on), pin Placket to centre front of Front and stitch around stitching lines, pivoting on needle at lower corners. Cut along centre front slash line through both layers of fabric, cutting diagonally into the corners, as indicated, but taking care not to cut the stitching. Press under 1cm on each long edge of Placket, then trim this back to 5mm. Pull the Placket through to the right side of the Shirt Front. Taking care not to catch the lower part of the Placket in the seam, fold one long edge of Placket in half along fold line and topstitch pressed edge in place over seam line. Repeat for second side of Placket. Lap left edge of Placket over right. Make sure that all raw edges on lower end of Placket are tucked to the wrong side, then topstitch across lower edge of Placket through all layers to secure.

Stitch Front to Back at shoulder seams. Press under 2cm on lower edge of each Sleeve and topstitch close to edge, then again, 2mm from first stitching.

Run a line of ease stitching around crown of each Sleeve, between dots. Stitch Sleeves to armholes, adjusting ease stitching if necessary.

Stitch sleeve and side seam in one continuous operation, matching sleeve seams.

For Collar, cut a piece of knit ribbing to fit around neck edge of shirt (excluding Plackets). If you are using the knit collar from an existing school polo shirt, cut a strip approximately 4cm wide. You can then trim strip to required length by cutting carefully between the vertical rows of ribbing – it will not fray if you do this. (If you are using purchased knit ribbing, you need to cut an 8cm-wide strip x the length of the neck edge, plus 1cm for seam allowance. Stitch the short ends together, allowing a 5mm seam, press seam allowance open. Fold band in half lengthwise, matching seams and press. You can now proceed as for the double knit collar.)

With right sides together and raw edges matching, baste Collar to neck edge of shirt. Cut a 2.5cm-wide bias strip of knit fabric to fit neck edge, plus extra for turning. With right sides together and raw edges even, stitch bias strip to neck edge through all layers, sandwiching Collar at the same time. Turn binding to inside, fold in raw ends at centre front to neaten and slipstitch in place. Press. Topstitch around neck edge, about 3mm from seam to prevent bias facing strip from rolling out.

Press under 2cm on lower edge of shirt and finish hem as for Sleeves.

Stitch buttons to front of Placket and stitch snap fasteners beneath to secure.

Using a fabric pen, trace or draw an approximation of your school's badge on the lefthand front of the shirt, if desired.

5 HAT Stitch centre back seam of Hat Side and press seam open. Press Side in half lengthwise, wrong sides together, matching centre back seams. Run a line of ease stitching around raw edges of Hat Side. With wrong sides facing, baste Hat Crowns together. With right sides together, baste and stitch Crown to raw edges (not folded edge) of Hat Side, pulling up ease stitching to accommodate fullness, and distributing fullness evenly so that there are no tucks in seam line. Topstitch around Hat Side, close to seam.

Join centre back seam of each Brim section and press seam open. Matching centre back seams, stitch Brims together around outer edge, trim seam, clip curves, turn right side out and press. Stitch raw edges of Brim together, following seam line. Topstitch around completed Brim, 1cm from the outer edge, then at 1cm intervals until you reach the centre. Clip across seam allowance to seam line stitching around inner edge of Brim.

With centre back seams aligned, position folded edge of Hat Side over inner edge of Brim, using stitching line as a guide, and stretching Brim to fit if necessary. Baste. Topstitch close to folded edge of Side. Neaten seam and press towards Side, then topstitch again, about 3-4mm from first stitching.

6 SHOES Stitch centre back seam of Shoe, stitching 2-3mm from edge. Stitch centre front seam, as far as small dot. With right sides together, stitch Sole into Shoe – you might find it easier to do this by hand as it's rather fiddly. Fold under seam allowance on lace edge of shoe and glue lightly in place. When glue has dried, use a tapestry needle to thread "laces" into shoes in a criss-cross fashion.

Paper Whirligigs
Page 53

Measurements

Each whirligig requires a 14cm square. Sails are about 20cm across at widest point.

Materials

- 30cm x 5mm dowel
- Brightly-coloured acrylic paint and paintbrush
- Two flat sheets of coloured wrapping paper
- Spray adhesive
- Transfer paper or dressmaker's carbon
- Skewer or large needle
- Craft glue
- Two small washers (see NOTE, below)
- Drawing pin

NOTE. Small washers are needed to allow the whirligig to spin freely. You can use light metal or plastic washers, available from hardware stores, or you can cut small circles from cardboard (trace around a coin) and punch a hole in the centre with a paper punch.

Method

1 DOWEL STICK Paint dowel stick with two coats of acrylic paint and allow to dry.

2 JOINING PAPERS Working in a well-ventilated area on a protected surface, spray the wrong side of each sheet of wrapping paper sparingly with spray adhesive and glue them together to give a double-sided sheet.

3 CUTTING Trace the pattern on the pattern sheet (in pink) and, using transfer paper, rule the outline of the square and trace over the cutting lines. Cut out square and carefully cut along internal cutting lines.

4 ASSEMBLY Use a skewer or large needle to make holes as indicated in points A, B, C and D. Turn points to the centre in alphabetical order, holding each in place with a tiny dab of craft glue.

Place a washer at front and back of centre and pin the whirligig to the top of the dowel stick with a drawing pin. Do not press the pin in too tightly or the whirligig won't spin.

Bath Mitts

Page 59

Measurements

Approximately 17cm across.

Materials

- Thin household sponge cloths: pink, orange, yellow, blue, turquoise
- Matching sewing thread
- Craft glue

Pattern pieces

All pattern pieces are printed on the pattern sheet in a grey tone. Trace Fish Body, Fin, Side Fin, Mouth, Eye, Pupil, Flower, Flower Centre, Crab Body, Claw, Leg and Spot.

Cutting

NOTE. All pattern pieces are actual size. There is no need to add seam allowance. Before cutting pattern pieces, remove sponges from packaging and leave overnight to stiffen slightly. This will make them easier to stitch.

FISH

From turquoise sponge, cut two Fish Bodies.

From blue sponge, cut two Fins and two Side Fins.

From orange sponge, cut two Mouths and ten Flower Centres.

From yellow sponge, cut two Eyes and four Flowers.

From pink sponge, cut two Pupils and six Flowers.

CRAB

From orange sponge, cut two Crab Bodies.

From yellow sponge, cut eight Legs, two Claws and two Eyes.

From pink sponge, cut twelve Spots.

From turquoise sponge, cut two Pupils.

Method

1 BODY DETAILS Using photograph as a guide, position appropriate body features (eyes, spots, flowers, side fins and fish mouth) onto right side of respective bodies and hold in place with a tiny dab of craft glue. The fish is patterned the same on both sides of its body. The crab has eyes on the front side only but spots on both sides

Using blanket stitch or a medium machine zigzag, attach each piece to body. When positioning the Flowers, stitch around the Centres only, through all layers, leaving the petals free. Stitch the Mouth in place on the fish only where it overlaps the Body.

Position top and bottom Fins on fish and Legs and Claws on crab, on wrong side of one Body piece, 6mm in from edge, and hold in place with a little glue.

2 JOINING BODIES Before stitching Bodies together, reinforce opening edges (between the back Legs on the crab and around the tail of the fish) on each Body section by

oversewing around the edges with blanket stitch or machine zigzag.

With wrong sides facing, blanket stitch or zigzag Bodies together around outer edges (including around Mouth of fish), sandwiching Legs, Claws and Fins and leaving a gap for openings.

3 STORAGE Store completed mitts in a sealed plastic bag to prevent their becoming too dry.

Furry Monster Purse

Page 48

Measurements

Approximately 10cm diameter.

Materials

◆ 12cm x 25cm novelty fur fabric
◆ 15cm metal zipper (see **Note**, below)
◆ Pair of 15mm-diameter joggle eyes
◆ Craft glue

NOTE. The teeth on a metal zip look more monster-like, but a nylon zip will do.

Pattern piece

Pattern piece is printed on pattern sheet in a grey tone. Trace Monster Purse.

Cutting

NOTE. Pattern piece includes 5mm seam allowance.

From fur fabric, cut two Monster Purses.

Method

1 DARTS With right sides together, stitch darts in both pieces. With small sharp scissors, snip across dart seam allowance towards point and finger press allowance open as far as possible.

2 ZIP Stitch zip to one edge of one purse section, between dots. Stitch remaining side of zip to corresponding edge of second Purse section, ensuring that darts are aligned.

3 JOINING SECTIONS Open zip slightly. With right sides together, stitch around raw edges from one end of zip to the other. Open zip and turn right side out.

4 EYES Glue joggle eyes in place on one side of purse, towards zip, as photographed.

Baby's Footy Boots

Page 58

Measurements

To fit age: 3 (6, 12) months. To fit foot length: approximately 8 (9.5, 12.5)cm. Length from ankle to sole: approximately 8 (10.5, 10.5)cm.

Materials

8-ply acrylic (we used Panda Disco), 20g balls:
◆ **Main Colour** (MC): 1 (1, 2) ball/s
◆ **Contrast Colour** (CC): 1 ball (all sizes)
◆ One pair each 3.25mm (No 10) and 4.00mm (No 8) knitting needles
◆ One 3.50mm crochet hook
◆ Knitter's needle for sewing seams

Tension

See **Knitting and Crochet Notes** on page 119. 22 sts and 30 rows to 10cm over st st, using 4.00mm needles.

FOOTBALL BOOTS
(make 2, beg at ankle)
Using CC and 3.25mm needles, cast on 26 (30, 34) sts.
Work 3 rows purl fabric (reverse st st), beg with a knit row (1st row is wrong side).
Change to 4.00mm needles and beg patt.
Using MC work 4 rows st st.
Using CC work 4 rows st st.
Using MC work 4 rows st st.
Sizes 6 and 12 months only. Rep last 8 rows once more.
All sizes. Break off MC.
Shape instep. Next row. Using CC K9 (11, 13), rejoin MC and knit 8 sts, *turn*.
Cont using MC on these centre 8 sts, leaving 9 (11, 13) sts unworked at each end, work 9 (13, 17) rows st st, beg and ending with a purl row, *turn*, break off yarn and leave these 8 sts on lefthand needle.
Shape sides. With right side facing, use CC at the end of the first group of 9 (11, 13) sts and knit up 7 (9, 12) sts evenly along first side of instep, knit across 8 sts from end of instep, knit up 7 (9, 12) sts evenly along other side of instep, then knit across rem 9 (11, 13) sts...40 (48, 58) sts.

Using CC work 3 rows st st, beg with a purl row.
Using MC work 4 rows st st.
Using CC knit one row, then work 3 rows purl fabric, beg with a knit row (1st row is wrong side).
Shape heel and toe. Using MC for rem, cont as folls:
1st row. K2tog, K16 (20, 25), (K2tog) twice, K16 (20, 25), K2tog...36 (44, 54) sts.
2nd and foll alt rows. Purl.
3rd row. K2tog, K14 (18, 23), (K2tog) twice, K14 (18, 23), K2tog...32 (40, 50) sts.
5th row. K2tog, K12 (16, 21), (K2tog) twice, K12 (16, 21), K2tog...28 (36, 46) sts.
6th row. Purl.
Size 3 months only. Cast off.
Sizes 6 and 12 months only. 7th row. K2tog, K(14, 19), (K2tog) twice, K(14, 19), K2tog...(32, 42) sts.
8th row. Purl.
Cast off.

BOOT STUDS (make 12)
Using CC and 3.25mm needles, cast on one st.
1st row. (K1, P1, K!, P1) all into next st, *turn*.
2nd row. P4, *turn*.
3rd row. Sl 2, K2tog, p2sso.
Fasten off, leaving a length of yarn to sew Boot Stud in position.

LACES (make 2)
Using CC and hook, make approximately 55cm of ch.
Fasten off and darn in ends.

To make up

Join ankle and foot seam. Sew six Boot Studs (in two lines of three) to MC section of each sole. Using a knitter's needle, thread laces in position across instep, forming two crosses and tying laces at ankle, as photographed.

Bunny Ear Slippers

Page 58

Measurements

To fit: 2-3 (4-5, 6) years. Fits foot: approximately 15 (17.5, 19)cm.

Materials

8-ply wool (we used Patons Fireside),
  50g balls:

- ◆ **Main Colour** (M, blue): 1 (2, 2) ball/s
- ◆ **1st Contrast** (C1, beige): 1 ball (all sizes)
- ◆ **2nd Contrast** (C2, cream): 1 ball (all sizes)
- ◆ Small quantity black yarn for embroidery
- ◆ One pair 3.00mm (No 11) knitting needles
- ◆ Knitter's needle for sewing seams and embroidery

Tension

See **Knitting and Crochet Notes** on page 119.
26 sts and 47 rows to 10cm over garter st,
using 3.00mm needles.

SLIPPERS (beg at heel)

Using M and 3.00mm needles, cast on 2 sts.
1st row. Knit.
2nd row. Inc one st in first st, K1.
**3rd and 4th rows. Knit.
5th row. Inc one st in first st, knit to end.**
Rep from ** to ** 8 times…12 sts.

NOTE. As there are 2 rows between incs, the inc sts will alternate from one side to the other, thus forming a triangle.

Next row. Cast on 11 (**13**, 15) sts, K11 (**13**, 15), P1, knit to last st, P1, *turn*, cast on 11 (**13**, 15) sts…34 (**38**, 42) sts.
Proceed as folls. **1st row.** Knit.
2nd row. K11 (**13**, 15), P1, K10, P1, K11 (**13**, 15).
Rep 1st and 2nd rows 17 (**22**, 26) times.
Next row. K2, (P1, K1) 5 (**6**, 7) times, K11, (P1, K1) 5 (**6**, 7) times, K1.
Next row. (K1, P1) 6 (**7**, 8) times, K10, (P1, K1) 6 (**7**, 8) times.
Rep last 2 rows 8 times.
Next row. *K2tog; rep from * to end…17 (**19**, 21) sts.
Next row. Purl.
Next row. *K2tog; rep from * to last st, K1…9 (**10**, 11) sts.
Break off yarn, run end through rem sts, draw up and fasten off securely.

BUNNY EARS (make 4)

Using C1 and 3.00mm needles, cast on 2 sts.
Knit 2 rows garter st.
Cont in garter st, inc one st at each end of next and foll 4th row…6 sts.
Knit 7 rows garter st.
Break off yarn, run end through rem sts, draw up and fasten off securely.

To make up

Using a flat seam, sew side edges of rib section tog to make toe of Slipper. Sew side edges of back triangle to cast-on sts at sides. Attach one pair of Ears to each Slipper, as shown.

Using black yarn, embroider eyes, nose and mouth below Ears as photographed. Using C2, make two small pompoms (see page 119) and sew one to back of each Slipper.

Knitted Balls

Page 58

Measurements

Circumference is approximately 37cm.

Materials

8-ply yarn (we used Hayfield Grampian DK),
  50g balls:

  BALL A (two colours)
- ◆ 1 ball yellow
- ◆ 1 ball red

  BALL B or C (horizontal stripes or multi-coloured segments)
- ◆ 1 ball blue
- ◆ 1 ball red
- ◆ 1 ball yellow
- ◆ 1 ball green
- ◆ 1 ball purple
- ◆ One pair 3.25mm (No 10) knitting needles
- ◆ Polyester fibrefill

BALL A

Segment (make 5)
Using yellow yarn, cast on 2 sts.

NOTE. Work in st st throughout.

Inc one st at each end of next 2 rows, at each end of foll 2 alt rows, then at each end of foll 3rd row…12 sts.
Work 2 rows.
Inc one st at each end of next row…14 sts.
Rep last 3 rows once…16 sts.
Work 5 rows.
Inc one st at each end of next row…18 sts.
Work 2 rows.
Change to red yarn.
Work 13 rows.
Change to yellow yarn.
Work 3 rows.

Dec one st at each end of next row…16 sts.
Work 5 rows.
Dec one st at each end of next row and foll 3rd row…12 sts.
Work 2 rows.
Dec one st at each end of next row…10 sts.
Rep last 3 rows once…8 sts.
Dec one st at each end of foll 2 alt rows, then at each end of next row…2 sts.
Next row. K2tog and fasten off.

To make up

Join sides of Segments neatly to form Ball, leaving an opening for filling. Fill firmly and close seam.

BALL B

Work as for Ball A, working in st st stripe patt of 4 rows each of blue, red, yellow, green and purple throughout.

BALL C

Work as for Ball A, working first Segment in blue only, second Segment in red only, third Segment in yellow only, fourth Segment in green only, and fifth Segment in purple only.

Furry Pencil Case

Page 61

Measurements

Approximately 12cm x 26cm.

Materials

- ◆ 28cm x 23cm novelty fur fabric
- ◆ 25cm zip

Method

1 ZIP With right sides together and allowing 1cm seams, insert zip between two long (28cm) sides of fur rectangle. Open zip slightly. Zip should fill upper edge of case entirely. If there is any gap at each end, stitch seams to close.

2 FINISHING With right sides together and allowing 1cm seams, stitch side seams. Open zip and turn right side out.

Furry Shoulder Bag

Page 61

Measurements

Approximately 35cm x 40cm.

Materials

◆ 0.4m x 112cm novelty fur fabric
◆ 1.1m x 2cm-wide grosgrain ribbon
◆ 25cm square contrast felt, for star
◆ 25cm square transparent plastic, for star
◆ Glitter
◆ Craft glue

Cutting

From fur fabric, cut two rectangles, each 35cm x 40cm.

Method

1 STAR Star outline is printed on pattern sheet in black. Trace onto felt square, but do not cut out. Place transparent plastic square on top of felt square and stitch around outline, through both layers, leaving one "arm" open. Sprinkle glitter into star outline between felt and plastic, then finish stitching last arm of star to enclose glitter completely. Trim around stitched outline about 3mm from stitching. Glue completed Star to centre of one fur rectangle.

2 BAG With right sides together, stitch rectangles together around sides and lower edge, allowing 1cm seams. Fold under 3cm on upper raw edge and topstitch in place, catching raw ends of ribbon strap in place inside on side seams at the same time.

Ham Bag

Page 68

Measurements

53cm x 47cm.

Materials

◆ 0.55m x 120cm calico
◆ Stencil film, such as Mylar
◆ Fine black felt-tipped pen
◆ Craft knife or scalpel
◆ Artist's acrylics in colours of your choice (we used Rust, Antique Blue and Metallic Gold)
◆ Fabric or textile medium
◆ Sponge
◆ Fabric pens in grey and brown, optional
◆ Small scrap of fabric for patch, optional
◆ Stranded embroidery cotton, optional
◆ 1.2m unbleached cotton cord

Method

1 PREPARATION Wash calico and press when dry. Cut a rectangle 49cm x 114cm. Fold rectangle in half crosswise, wrong sides together and finger-press to mark lower fold. Open fabric out flat again.

2 CUTTING STENCIL Stencil outlines are printed on pattern sheet in a pink tone. Trace onto stencil film with a felt-tipped marker and cut out carefully with a craft knife or scalpel.

3 APPLYING STENCIL With casing, seam allowance and lower edge in mind, position stencil on centre front of bag. Mix paint with textile medium according to the manufacturer's instructions and, using a fairly dry sponge, apply design to bag. We used Rust for pig and lettering, then a very sparse coat of Metallic Gold for pig only. Hearts were stencilled in Antique Blue. When design is complete, carefully remove stencil and allow to dry. If desired, outline motifs and lettering with fabric pen to give a crisper edge. Heat set paint with an iron, following manufacturer's instructions.

If desired, cut a small rectangular patch, about 4cm x 6cm, and stitch to pig with embroidery cotton, using rustic stitching.

4 BAG Fold stencilled rectangle in half crosswise, right sides together, and stitch side seams, allowing 1cm seam allowance and leaving a gap of 1.5cm in one side seam, precisely 5cm from top edge.

Press under 5mm on top raw edge, then press under another 3.5cm, and stitch close to inner edge, forming casing. Stitch again close to upper edge. Turn bag

Thread cotton cor casing and knot ends.

Baby Santa

Page 69

Measurements

Approximately 25cm .

Materials

◆ 30cm x 60cm red fabric
◆ 20cm x 25cm white fabric
◆ 10cm x 30cm strip black fabric
◆ Double-sided inter such as Vliesofix
◆ Machine thread: red, white, yellow, black
◆ Purchased white 12mm bias binding

Pattern piece

Pattern piece is printed on pattern sheet in pink. Trace one Bib. Trace Belt and Beard from pattern piece onto Vliesofix and cut out, leaving approximately 6mm around traced line.

Cutting

NOTE. 6mm seam allowance is **included** on Bib outline, except at neckline, where it is not needed as the edge is bound. Do not add seam allowance to appliqué outlines.

From red fabric, cut two Bibs.

Apply traced Vliesofix Beard to wrong side of white fabric and cut out accurately.

Apply traced Vliesofix Belt to wrong side of black fabric and cut out accurately.

Method

1 APPLIQUÉ Remove backing paper from Beard and place onto right side of one red Bib piece, matching neck edges. Fuse in place with an iron. Fuse Belt to Bib front in the same way, using pattern piece as guide to position.

Set machine to a close zigzag and machine stitch around scalloped edge of Beard, using white thread. Using black thread, appliqué Belt in position in the same way. Finally, change to yellow thread and, referring to photograph as a guide, stitch a buckle on the centre of the Belt.

2 BIB With right sides facing, stitch Bibs together, leaving neck edge open. Clip curves, turn right side out and press.

3 BINDING & TIES Cut a 1m length of bias binding and finger press to mark halfway point. Open out one edge of binding and, with right side of binding facing underside of Bib, raw edges even and centre mark of binding placed at centre of neck edge, pin binding to neck edge of Bib and stitch around neck edge only. Excess binding should extend at each end of neck edge to form ties.

Fold remaining edge of binding to front of Bib, folding edges of ties together at the same time. Fold in raw ends of ties, then topstitch edges of binding together, stitching along edge of tie, around neck edge, and along edge of remaining tie to finish.

Potted Pomander

Page 68

Materials

- ◆ Medium-sized, thin-skinned orange
- ◆ Whole cloves (see NOTE, below)
- ◆ Fine skewer or large needle
- ◆ Orris root powder (from craft stores)
- ◆ 7cm-high terracotta pot, 8cm-diameter
- ◆ Scraps of felt in several colours
- ◆ Contrast embroidery cotton
- ◆ Small amount polyester fibrefill
- ◆ Craft glue
- ◆ Wooden satay stick

NOTE. If making several pomanders, cloves can be bought in bulk in Asian food stores and in craft stores selling pot-pourri supplies.

Pattern pieces

Pattern pieces for bird are printed on this page. Trace Body, Wing, Tail and Beak.

Cutting

NOTE. Pieces are actual size. Do not add seam allowance.

From felt in main colour, cut two Bodies.

From contrasting colour, cut two Wings.
From contrasting scraps, cut three Tails and two Beaks.

Method

1 POMANDER Pierce the skin of the orange with a fine skewer or large needle and stick whole cloves into skin, working out in a tight spiral from the bottom until whole orange is closely covered. If possible, choose cloves that still have the little round seed head attached to the star-shaped stalk – they look nicer.

Roll the completed pomander in orris root powder and tap off excess. Pomanders can be made up to several months before they are required and left in an airy place to dry out. The orange will dry completely, becoming smaller and harder, but will not rot because of the preservative quality of the cloves and orris root.

2 BIRD Using a little craft glue, stick a Wing to right side of each Body. Stick rim of each Beak to inside edge of head, and stick the three Tail feathers, overlapping each other, to wrong side of one Body so that they will protrude, as pictured. Allow glue to dry before sewing.

Using two strands of contrast embroidery thread, work a satin stitch eye (see **Embroidery Stitch Guide** on page 119) on each side of head and work two long stitches on each Wing, as photographed.

With wrong sides facing, place Bodies together and work small neat blanket stitch around outer edges, leaving a narrow opening in lower edge for filling. Stuff with a small amount of fibrefill and stitch opening closed. Glue Beaks together.

3 ASSEMBLY Push a satay stick through bird from seam in top of back, to emerge through seam at bottom. Push spike of stick into pomander, then break off remaining stick, flush with top of back so that it can't be seen.

Place bird-topped pomander into terracotta pot.

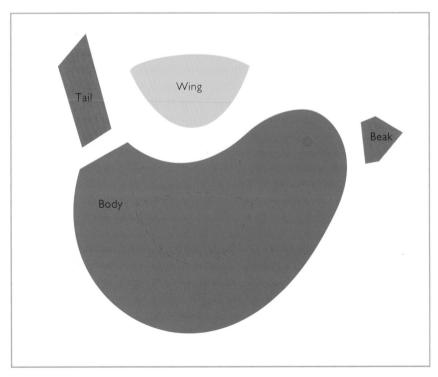